ALSO BY BOB ROTELLA

The Unstoppable Golfer
The Golfer's Mind
Your 15th Club
Putting Out of Your Mind
Life Is Not a Game of Perfect
The Golf of Your Dreams
Golf Is a Game of Confidence
Golf Is Not a Game of Perfect

HOW
CHAMPIONS
THINK

In Sports and in Life

DR. BOB ROTELLA

WITH BOB CULLEN

SIMON & SCHUSTER

NEW YORK   LONDON   TORONTO   SYDNEY   NEW DELHI

Simon & Schuster
1230 Avenue of the Americas
New York, NY 10020

First Simon & Schuster hardcover edition May 2015

SIMON & SCHUSTER and colophon are registered
trademarks of Simon & Schuster, Inc.

For information about special discounts for bulk
purchases, please contact Simon & Schuster Special Sales at
1-866-506-1949 or business@simonandschuster.com.

The Simon & Schuster Speakers Bureau can bring authors
to your live event. For more information or to book an
event, contact the Simon & Schuster Speakers Bureau at
1-866-248-3049 or visit our website at www.simonspeakers.com.

Manufactured in the United States of America

1   3   5   7   9   10   8   6   4   2

Library of Congress Cataloging-in-Publication Data is available.

ISBN 978-1-4767-8862-3
ISBN 978-1-4767-8865-4 (ebook)

To Dad, for being the greatest husband, father, father-in-law, grandfather, and great-grandfather any man could ever hope to be. And to his great-grandchildren, my grandchildren, Lucy, Max, Laura, Thomas, and George, and to all my nieces and nephews, wishing each of you a wonderful life, going for your dreams with passion and enthusiasm.

CONTENTS

HOW
CHAMPIONS
THINK

1.

What LeBron James Has in Common with Pat Bradley

HAVE BEEN privileged to spend my life helping people who want to be exceptional. A desire to be exceptional may not in itself strike you as unusual. Everyone, as a kid, has daydreams in which he catches the touchdown pass as time expires to win the Super Bowl, or she pole-vaults sixteen feet to win an Olympic gold medal. But I'm not talking about daydreams or about the unrealized fantasies of many adults. I'm talking about a desire so fierce that it changes a person's life. Exceptional people begin with just such ambitions. From them, I've learned how a champion's thoughts are different from the thoughts of most people. That difference is what this book is about.

I've worked with the winners of eighty-four major golf championships on the men's, women's, and senior tours. I've worked with Olympic gold medalists in the equestrian sports. I've worked with NCAA champions in track and field, soccer, lacrosse, and basketball. I've worked with winners of major tennis tournaments. Three of the five players in the history of the PGA Tour to shoot a competitive 59—Chip Beck, David Duval, and Jim Furyk—were working with me when they did it. I've worked with exceptionally successful people in the entertainment and business worlds. Each of them has taught me something about the minds of exceptional people.

They have confirmed my belief that the ideas people choose to have about themselves largely determine the quality of the lives they lead. We can choose to believe in ourselves, and thus to strive, to risk, to persevere, and to achieve. Or we can choose to cling to security and mediocrity. We can choose to set no limits on ourselves, to set high goals and dream big dreams. We can use those dreams to fuel our spirits with passion. Or we can become philosophers of the worst kind, inventing ways to rationalize our failures, inventing excuses for mediocrity. We can fall in love with our own abilities and our own potential, then choose to maximize those abilities. Or we can decide that we have no special talents or abilities and try to be happy being safe and comfortable.

As I've worked, I've been troubled at times by the realization that the champions I know are becoming more atypical—*too* exceptional, if you will. Our grandparents and great-grandparents migrated and struggled for many years to give us the freedom we now have, a precious birthright. We're free to choose what we're going to think about ourselves. No one can stop us from chasing our dreams. Yet many people today choose to squander this birthright. They choose to believe that because of where they were born or who their parents are, they don't have a fair chance in life. They're choosing to believe that the competition—from America and around the world—is just too tough. They're choosing to believe in someone else's talent more than their own. They're choosing to be mediocre.

I'm always telling people that I don't care what their families or their schools or their communities said or thought about them. I tell them, "You're an adult now, and you get to decide." So what's the decision going to be? You get to write your life story. Will you be heroic or just someone trying to get by? Will you be the star or someone sitting on the end of the bench?

I have no trouble with someone who strives to be the best and finishes in the middle of the pack. There's honor in that. I don't see that person as a failure. To the contrary, he will come to the end of his days with a smile on his face, because he spent the time and talent God gave him having a ball, finding out how good he could get. He will not be the person who goes to the grave thinking, "If only I'd been as talented as, say, LeBron James! My life would have been great!"

In fact, such a person doesn't have an inkling of the most important talent LeBron James has. Nor does he know he could have chosen to have that talent himself. I know, because I've heard about it from the source.

Some years ago, I got a call from Lance Blanks, who was then the assistant general manager of the NBA's Cleveland Cavaliers. I'd known Lance since his days as a basketball player for the University of Virginia, where I taught and helped the athletic program as a sports psychologist. Lance wanted to know if I would spend a day talking with LeBron, then (and now again) the cornerstone of Cleveland's franchise. I was happy to say yes.

I knew something about LeBron, of course. I knew the outer dimensions. He was six-eight, weighed two hundred fifty chiseled pounds, and had explosive speed. I knew he had been perhaps the most publicized high school basketball player since Kareem Abdul-Jabbar was known as Lew Alcindor. I knew he'd been the NBA's number one draft choice the year he finished high school and I knew he'd been a very successful professional for the Cavaliers. But until I had a chance to talk to him, I didn't know the most important thing about LeBron.

"I want to be the greatest basketball player in history," he told me.

"Beautiful," I thought. "This is a truly talented guy."

It was not that he had the physical gifts. It was LeBron's mind.

I've been encountering his kind of attitude on occasion for more than three decades, and when I have encountered it, I have almost always had the pleasure of working with someone truly exceptional. One of my first clients in this category was someone who could hardly have been physically more different from LeBron, professional golfer Pat Bradley. Pat had average size and average clubhead speed; nothing about her initial appearance would suggest athletic ability to most people. And that was not even the most significant difference. LeBron had been a prodigy of whom much was expected from the time he was maybe fourteen years old. Pat had grown up in golfing obscurity. She was a girl from New England, which is not a cradle of golfers because of the short golf season up north. She hadn't gone to one of the colleges that traditionally has a strong women's golf team. LeBron would have disappointed a lot of people if he hadn't made himself into a great basketball player. Pat, had she been mediocre, would only have confirmed people's expectations. When I met her, she'd been a professional golfer for eleven years, and she'd won one tournament.

I asked her about her dreams and goals.

Almost diffidently, Pat said she wanted to win the LPGA Player of the Year award. She wanted to have the tour's lowest scoring average. She wanted to win all of the women's major championships. And she wanted to make the LPGA Hall of Fame. At the time, an LPGA player had to win thirty tournaments, including two majors, to be eligible for the Hall of Fame. It was the highest Hall of Fame hurdle in sports.

She asked me if I thought she could do these things.

I said, "I don't know if you can do them, but I'm excited to work with someone who has your dreams."

In the next ten years or so, Pat achieved all of those goals. So I certainly didn't discourage LeBron from thinking he could be the greatest. I just asked him where he thought he stood with regard to that goal.

Sometimes, when I ask a client this kind of question, I'll get a response that indicates a troubled mind. A golfer might say that he's got the yips with his putter or his wedges. A singer might say she has stage fright. A businessperson might say that he's freezing up when he makes sales calls. Initially, LeBron's response was less about his mind than about his skills.

"I'm pretty darn good," LeBron said, "but I'm not going to become the greatest basketball player in history if my teams don't win championships, and my teams aren't going to become champions if I don't become a better three-point shooter." (It tends to be forgotten now, but LeBron was not a finished player when he entered the NBA. He made only 29 percent of his three-point attempts in his rookie season.) "Right now, when I get into the playoffs, other teams know that I can't make the three, so they won't even guard me. They just look at me and talk trash to me and say, 'Go ahead and take it. We know you can't make it and you know you can't make it.' "

I wasn't surprised to hear that opposing players would talk trash with LeBron, or that it would bother him. I've worked with enough athletes to know that the godlike images we're fed by the media can often disguise reality. Superstars have doubts and fears just like the rest of us. So I nodded, and LeBron went on.

"I've started to think a little bit on my threes," he acknowledged. "You know, I have some doubt about it."

Yes, I knew. In basketball, as in golf, as in almost any sport involving motor skills, an athlete gets the best results when he *doesn't* think. Once an athlete has learned a skill—as LeBron had learned to shoot a basketball—he needs to trust that skill, focus on the target, and let the shot go without thinking about how to do it or being concerned about the result. In slightly more scientific terms, the subconscious areas of our minds do the best job of controlling motor skills. When the conscious brain gets involved, our bodies tend to become awkward. Doubt has a way of turning on that conscious brain, which is why confident shooters are better than shooters who lack confidence. A great deal of my work with athletes revolves around teaching them how to keep the conscious mind inactive or quiet when they're performing.

It may surprise some readers to learn that the suggestions I gave to LeBron involved a lot more of what most people would perceive as plain hard work than they involved what most people would consider sports psychology.

I did tell him that I thought he could benefit from one of the standard methods of sports psychology, visualization. I wanted him to see himself making three-point shots. I suggested that he ask the Cavaliers' staff to make a highlight video for him, about eight to twelve minutes long. This video would be a LeBron James long-range shooting montage. It would have LeBron making threes off the dribble. It would show LeBron catching the ball and making threes spotting up. It could have some of LeBron's favorite music in the background, helping him to attach the good feelings associated with that music to the act of shooting threes. He would watch it every night. As he fell asleep, he could conjure up images of himself making three-point shots against tall, quick, tenacious defenders. He could let them fill his dreams.

All of this would help him improve his three-point shooting, because it would feed the right sorts of images to his subconscious, helping him become a more trusting, confident shooter. But if improvement were as easy as watching videos, the NBA would have a lot more great three-point shooters. It isn't. The mental game is a big part of sport, but it must be combined with physical competence.

So I suggested that LeBron hire a shooting coach and work with that coach every day. I told him he needed to make maybe two hundred three-point shots off the dribble every day, imagining the best defender in the league guarding him. I told him he needed to make another two hundred catch-and-shoot three-pointers. I told him I didn't care how many shots it took to make those four hundred three-pointers, or how long it took. If he wanted to be great, he would find the time and find the energy. The actual number of shots I suggested was not as important, in my mind, as the idea that LeBron would set a practice goal for himself, commit to achieving it every day, and wait patiently for results.

I told him patience was essential because I had no way of predicting how long it would take to see improvement in his shooting statistics if he took my suggestions. But the patience and tenacity required were factors that could help him separate himself from his peers. A lot of athletes might undertake an improvement regimen like the one I suggested to LeBron. But not many would stick with it. After a few weeks, if they weren't seeing immediate results, they'd find a reason to quit. Maybe they'd decide the extra practice was wearing them down. Maybe they'd decide that they just didn't have the talent to be a great outside shooter. They'd find a way to talk themselves out of it. To encourage LeBron to persevere, I told him about my belief that great basketball shooters, like great golfers and great baseball hitters, are for the most part made rather than born.

He and Pat Bradley had hard work in common. Pat didn't make it to the LPGA Tour Hall of Fame just because she wanted to. She used that desire to fuel hours and weeks and years of dedication and practice. Her dreams were her starting point.

With LeBron, I also talked a lot about Bill Russell and Michael Jordan. Unlike golf, basketball is a team game. An essential part of being a great player is, in my mind, playing and conducting yourself in ways that make your teammates better. That, far more than scoring average, is the hallmark of a truly great player. Jordan and Russell were the players LeBron was chasing, because in addition to being great individually, they were players whose teams won many championships. They were great leaders. I suggested that LeBron read about Russell and Jordan and talk to them about leadership whenever he had the chance.

I was very impressed with LeBron James. He was attentive. He asked insightful questions. It was clear that he was disciplined and that he set very high standards for himself. He was more than just a superstar. He was a very coachable athlete on a mission to see how great he could become. I gave him the suggestions I did because I knew that his desire to be the best would empower him. The way he chose to think about himself would drive him through the workouts, the visualization exercises, and all the other things he needed to do to improve. That's why the way he saw himself was his most important talent.

I have noticed a few things since I spoke with LeBron. One is that his three-point shooting has improved dramatically. It's now roughly 40 percent, a one-third improvement over his rookie year. And I noticed, of course, that he switched teams, giving himself a better chance to win championships. And I have no doubt that the success LeBron has enjoyed is due to the kind of hard work we talked about that day, to his dedication to improvement, and to his strong commitment to team success.

True superstars share his attitude. Not long after I worked with LeBron, I met with the University of Memphis basketball team, then coached by John Calipari and led on the floor by All-American Derrick Rose. I shared with the players how important I thought LeBron's attitude was in his success. A little while later, I got a call from Derrick. He had something he wanted to tell me. "Doc, I want to be the greatest basketball player in history," he said.

Derrick went on in 2011 to become the youngest MVP in the history of the NBA. He's suffered some devastating injuries in the last few years, and he's still working very hard to complete his rehabilitation from the subsequent knee surgeries. But if he does manage to heal fully, I'd advise LeBron and anyone else in the NBA to look out for him. Derrick, like LeBron and Pat Bradley, has the champion's first requirement—the attitude he's chosen, the way he's decided to see himself.

The vital importance of that sort of attitude is the foremost thing I have learned about exceptionalism in my decades of work with people striving to be great. Talent, conventionally defined, is of course part of the equation. As Bear Bryant once said, "When was the last time you saw a jackass win the Kentucky Derby?" But there are many people with physical talent, just as there are many people with raw intelligence. I would venture that most people are talented in something, whether they realize it or not. What sets merely talented people apart from exceptional people can't be measured by vertical leap, or time for the forty-yard dash, or length off the tee, or IQ. It's something internal. Great performers share a way of thinking, a set of attitudes and attributes like optimism, confidence, persistence, and strong will. They all want to push themselves to see how great they can become. These attributes and attitudes cause champions to work harder and smarter than other people as they prepare for competition. They help them stay focused under pressure and to produce their best performances when the stakes are highest.

I am hardly the first observer to notice this. In the Book of Ecclesiastes, it was written that the runner with the best foot speed doesn't always win the race and the strongest warrior doesn't always win the battle. That knowledge persisted into the twentieth century, but the reasons behind it remained obscure. Good coaches pondered it.

When I was a kid, I loved to hang out with such coaches. I had a cousin, Sal Somma, who was the football coach for many decades at New Dorp High School in New York. (There's a street named for him near the high school.) He was a friend and disciple of Vince Lombardi, whose coaching career began not far from New Dorp, at St. Cecilia High School in Englewood, New Jersey. When Sal would visit us in Vermont during school vacations, and when I sat and talked with other coaches, I became aware of the distinction between a "practice player" and a "gamer." Coaches like Sal loved to talk about what distinguished practice players (the failed runner with the best foot speed or the failed warrior with the greatest strength) from gamers. They knew that winning depended on identifying and developing gamers, and they tried intuitive ways to do it. They might run punishing preseason practices in the summer heat, counting on the practice players to quit and the gamers to identify themselves by their tenacity. They might try pep talks. They might paper their locker rooms with messages about hard work and dedication. John Wooden, during a career that started in the 1920s, thought long and hard about the nature of success and developed a "Pyramid of Success" that he taught to his UCLA basketball teams. All of those things might work, especially in the hands of a master coach and recruiter like Wooden, who won ten NCAA championships. Or they might not work.

At the time, the term "sports psychologist" had yet to be coined. And, in fact, a lot of great athletes from that era, if asked, didn't think it needed to be coined. I remember some years ago my friend Jim Lefebvre, the great ex-Dodger infielder, big league manager, and hitting coach, introduced me to Bob Gibson, the Hall of Fame pitcher of the 1960s and '70s for the St. Louis Cardinals. When Jim told Gibson what I did for a living, Gibson looked at me with what I think was an approximation of the scornful glare he used to direct at hitters.

"We didn't need sports psychology when I was playing," he said.

"Why was that?" I asked.

"Because when I was playing, if anyone ever thought about digging in at the plate, I'd hit him in the head. That was my sports psychology."

Jim and I laughed, the tentative laugh of people who hope, but are not certain, that what they've just heard was meant as a joke.

"Today if you did that they'd throw you out of the game and suspend you," Gibson said. "Hell, if I was pitching today I'd probably need a sports psychologist, too."

I think it was only a coincidence, though, that sports psychology began to emerge as a distinct discipline around the time Gibson retired and baseball tightened its rules against beanballs. Its emergence had more to do with the will to win. Coaches and athletes want to win so much that they're constantly looking for ways to get better. Around 1980, they started giving sports psychologists a chance to help their teams improve. That was the way I got started at the University of Virginia, after I got my PhD and joined the faculty there. The results were impressive enough that today, most every major college athletic program, and a lot of professional teams, has a sports psychologist or two on the staff.

Over time, the discipline has spread into other endeavors, where it's more broadly known as performance psychology. I spend a lot of my time counseling people whose only exposure to athletics might be an occasional round of golf or bowling. They're businessmen or singers or any of a hundred things. But they have performance issues just as athletes do, and the same ideas that help athletes improve can help them.

I don't think it's any coincidence that sports psychology emerged first in America, because I think of it as deeply rooted in the American psyche and the American culture, at least as that culture used to be. My grandparents, like the forebears of millions of people, came to America with little or nothing. They didn't choose America because they wanted anything handed to them or given to them. They just wanted to be in a place where, if they worked hard and had some good ideas, they could rise to the middle class or even higher. They wanted to be in a place where no one was going to stop them because of their last name or their father's station in life. Performance psychology fits neatly into that ethos.

Striving to be exceptional is never easy. But when people tell me that what I'm suggesting they do won't be easy, I just say, "You're right!" Going after big ideas takes sweat. It takes persistence, patience, and a bedrock belief in yourself. Not everyone will do it. That's why we call it trying to be exceptional.

I never, by the way, try to define "exceptional" for a client. For some of the people I work with, it may be defined by championships won. For others, it may be defined by money earned and the things that money can buy. For some people, it might be defined by a helping career in which they save souls or teach impoverished kids. I don't care *what* a person's dreams are. I care about *how* a person lives his life.

I care about whether a person refuses to place limits on himself and instead chases greatness. If a golfer tells me that his goal is maintaining his playing privileges by finishing in the top 125 on the PGA Tour, I'll challenge him. "Who are the one hundred twenty-four players you think are better than you, and why?" If someone tells me she's going to be an entrepreneur, I don't want to hear that she dreams of merely making a living. I want her to have extravagant dreams, to dream of creating a wildly successful, innovative company that will give wealth to her and her family and good jobs to many more people. If he wants to be a teacher, I don't want to hear that he aspires to get tenure, punch a clock for three decades, and retire in modest comfort. I want to hear that he has a passion to use his life and his talents giving hundreds, or thousands, of kids a better start in life. I want to help people like that.

I do it by teaching the attitudes and habits of an exceptional life. I teach what champions think. Whatever a person's aspirations might be, these qualities and these ways of thinking will support those aspirations. They'll help him keep his commitments and persist in working to improve. They'll help her come through in the clutch and overcome setbacks. They'll help him respond effectively to competition. They're not a mystery. They're not something that's either in your genes or not in your genes, like blue eyes. They can be learned. They're what this book is about.

The first essential quality is optimism.

2.

Learning to Be Optimistic

I HAD A privileged upbringing.

It wasn't that the Rotella family had a lot of money. We didn't. We were never hungry, but a lot of the food on our table consisted of vegetables we grew ourselves.

When I say I was privileged, I mean that my childhood taught me to be optimistic. I didn't know it then, but I realize now that this was a precious gift. Exceptional people, I have found, either start out being optimistic or learn to be optimistic because they realize that they can't get what they want in life without being optimistic. That's why I say I was privileged. I didn't have to learn optimism. It was given to me.

I don't mean that my mother and father, in the manner of some of today's parents, ever worried about my self-esteem. They didn't. They didn't praise me unless I did something praiseworthy. To the contrary, if I did less than my best at something, I got no credit for making a halfhearted effort. If my chore for the day was cutting the grass, and I didn't complete the job with neat edges, I did it over when my dad came home. I remember a day when I was working with my father to fix some window trim. I was nailing it in, and I hit a nail incorrectly and bent it. I was about to just pound the bent nail in, but when you bend a nail, the sound is quite different from that of a nail being struck properly and driven in straight. My dad was about ten yards away, and he heard it. Before I could continue, he came over to me and said, "What are you doing? You think we're going to paint over a bent nail? That's going to be your finished product? How can you live with that?"

I pulled out the bent nail and started over.

My dad believed passionately, and still believes, in education. It was an attitude he got from his father and the community he grew up in. He taught me that America is a great place for anyone who gets an education and takes advantage of it. He insisted that we do as well as possible in school. That usually meant As, though if he was persuaded that we were doing our best in a subject that was difficult for us, he would tolerate a B. He never told us what to do with our lives. He just taught us that we could do anything we wanted if we got an education, set our minds to it, and did our best. I learned to believe that with hard work, you *could* be the best.

That's optimism.

It may not be as natural for people growing up today to feel optimistic as it was for me and many others in my generation. Instead of seeing examples of people succeeding and progressing, they can find it all too easy to see examples of people struggling. Sometimes, when I'm visiting my hometown of Rutland, Vermont, I'm asked to speak to groups of young people. I remember a girl recently asking me, "How do you get to work with all of these great athletes? People from Rutland don't get to do that."

Her question was not unreasonable. One of the ways people learn to be optimistic is by seeking out role models who have achieved great things. If these role models are in some way similar to themselves, they can help instill optimism.

One classic example is the evolution of the world record for the one-mile run. For decades, the mark hovered at a second or two over four minutes. Pessimism abounded about whether a human being was even capable of running a four-minute mile. There were articles in the press in which supposed experts opined that the human body simply wasn't built to run a mile that fast. Then a British medical student and elite amateur runner, Roger Bannister, took a look at the prevailing pessimism and decided it was poppycock. Bannister decided he was capable of running a four-minute mile and he trained hard to do so. On a rainy day in 1954, he did it, running 3:59.4.

Almost immediately, an Australian runner, John Landy, bettered Bannister's record. Within a few years, many runners broke through the once-impregnable four-minute barrier. Bannister had been a powerful role model, and his success turned many runners from pessimists to optimists about their ability to break four minutes in the mile run.

I've seen the same sort of phenomenon in golf. When Padraig Harrington was growing up, no Irish golfer in memory had won a major championship. Padraig was and is exceptional in many ways, among them the fact that he didn't let this dearth of Irish role models deter him. Padraig broke through at the Open Championship in 2007, then won two more majors in 2008. Within four years, three more Irishmen followed him in winning majors—Graeme McDowell, Rory McIlroy, and Darren Clarke. It was no coincidence.

None of that, I suspect, was known to the girl in Rutland who didn't see any local role models.

"There are a lot of great people who have come from Rutland," I said.

"I don't know of any," the girl replied.

I told her that when I was growing up, I played basketball every day at a recreation center named for Andrea Mead Lawrence, who won two gold medals in alpine skiing at the 1952 Winter Olympics. (The rec center, alas, has been torn down.)

"I never heard of her," the girl said.

I told her that Andrea Mead Lawrence was only one of many people from Rutland who have become highly successful in sport and other activities. I said that if the girl had really wanted to find a role model from Rutland whose example she could follow to optimism and success, she would have found one.

The fact that she hadn't speaks, I think, to the pessimism that has infected many American communities. Sometimes, after I give a talk, parents will approach me and say that they wish their kids had been present to hear it. Then they'll catch themselves and say, "Maybe it's just as well. I wouldn't want them to get big dreams, then be discouraged when they can't achieve them."

I can't help but think that these parents are going to raise the sort of people who, whatever their dreams might have been at the age of fifteen, will by forty be people who just want to be safe and secure, who don't want a boss telling them they can produce more and earn more. That's the attitude that pessimism instills.

I don't believe that people are born either optimistic or pessimistic, the way they're born either right-handed or left-handed. Optimism is an attitude that people can choose to have. Obviously, I was fortunate in that my upbringing made it easier to be optimistic. But if it hadn't, I could have chosen optimism.

A kid today might have to look outside his hometown to find role models. The girl who questioned me could find examples of women from small cities like Rutland who have risen from modest circumstances to fulfill their dreams. Or she could persuade herself that she'd be the pioneer, that she'd be the first Rutland kid to achieve some wonderful dream and that she'd be a role model for others.

It's not easy, but it can be done. Successful people I have worked with do it all the time. They choose optimism. Whatever happens to them, they find reason to be hopeful.

Padraig Harrington chose optimism in that way. I remember one year at the Masters, before he won those majors, Padraig missed the cut. He played well, but he got some bad breaks. Good approach shots seemed to trickle off greens. Good putts lipped out. When I saw Padraig after the second round I was concerned that he'd be down and discouraged. I shouldn't have been. Some players would have decided that what happened to them was somehow evidence that they weren't cut out to win majors, or that Augusta National didn't suit their games, or that they were somehow jinxed. Not Padraig.

"I now know that I can win a major championship," Padraig told me. "On every shot I played this week, I had my mind where it needed to be. I was in the present, focused on that shot. I had a clear picture in my mind of what I wanted each ball to do. I know now I can quiet my mind and emotions and let my body do what it knows how to do under major tournament pressure. I'm so pleased I could do that in a tournament like this. Now I know I can accomplish these dreams of mine."

Optimism is often an act of faith, a belief in something that cannot be proven. Padraig had it. Anyone can have it.

I'm not saying that optimism won those three major titles for Padraig. He won them because he has talent and he worked very hard for many years to hone that talent. But Padraig's optimism helped him find the will to keep working through all the setbacks he had—and a golfer loses far more tournaments than he wins. His is a constant kind of optimism, and it works for him the way fertilizer works for flowers, enabling and enhancing all the efforts he makes to improve his game.

People like Padraig either consciously or unconsciously find ways to become and stay optimistic. Regardless of what happens to them in life—from the circumstances of their birth to a setback in a golf tournament—they find something hopeful. They find a reason to keep believing in themselves, to keep working hard. Optimism is a feeling they create for themselves.

Smart coaches have always understood the importance of optimism. I recall the way John Calipari handled his 2012 national championship team at the University of Kentucky. One of the key players on that team was guard Doron Lamb. The Wildcats needed his outside shooting to make their opponents play honest defense instead of collapsing around the basket. Doron did not have a good game in the semifinals against Louisville; he made less than half his shots and scored only ten points. I was helping John that year, and we both knew that Kansas, Kentucky's opponent in the finals, would likely play a defense designed to make it hard for Kentucky center Anthony Davis to score.

John normally runs very tough practices. He needs to be demanding with his players because so many of them are talented enough that the NBA drafts them long before they finish college. John has them only a year or two, and in that time has to remold them from high school hotshots to kids who dive on the floor after loose balls, play tenacious defense, and put the team's needs over their personal stats. Consequently, John is not often inclined to mince words in practice. When someone's not giving the effort John demands, John tells him about it in no uncertain terms.

But John recognized that with only two days between the semifinals and the final, Doron did not need to hear criticism. I watched him plant optimistic seed after optimistic seed in Doron's mind during the two practices Kentucky held prior to the final game.

"You practice hard and you'll have one of the best nights of your life," John told him. "You're going for thirty [points] and you're going to be the deciding factor and it's going to be the best game of your life to do it in." I could see Doron liked the idea.

On the night of the finals, Doron Lamb made his first two shots and Kentucky was off and running. He didn't get thirty points that night, but he got twenty-two and led the Wildcats in scoring as they won the 2012 NCAA Championship.

Again, optimism didn't put those points on the board. As with Padraig Harrington, Doron's success was built on talent and years of practice. But I don't know that he would have taken those first two shots, or made them, had John not helped him attain an optimistic attitude before the game.

That sort of situational optimism works particularly well when it's applied to motor skills like shooting a basketball or putting a golf ball. As I've said, shooting and putting are skills that, once learned, are best left to the subconscious part of the brain. Somewhere in that portion of your mind lie the places that most efficiently control learned body movements. When we're optimistic, we tend to let those subconscious brain elements do their work. Balls go into the basket. Putts fall into the hole.

It's no coincidence that Phil Mickelson has been a highly successful, exciting golfer, and that he likes to say, "The birdies are in the woods." What Phil means is that he remains optimistic even when he drives the ball off line, into the woods or rough instead of onto the fairway. That optimism is one reason he sometimes hits amazing recovery shots, like the one he hit off the pine straw to the 13th green en route to taking the 2010 Masters.

The opposite of this sort of situational optimism is an attitude of fear, concern, and doubt. In a word, pessimism. Pessimism tends to rouse the conscious brain and get it engaged. Our minds are programmed to work that way. In certain kinds of difficult situations, it helps to think things out calmly and rationally. The conscious mind is good for higher-level thinking; I wouldn't want my financial consultant, for instance, to pick investments for me without engaging it. But the conscious mind isn't good for shooting or putting. It tends to make basketball players and golfers move stiffly and awkwardly. Balls clank off the rim and putts lurch past the hole.

I like anyone who's performing to have an optimistic attitude, because performances go best when the performer trusts her skills and lets the performance flow. One tip I've shared with many golfers is a simple one: smile a little bit before each putt. Frowning is something your body does automatically when you've engaged your conscious mind to concentrate on a problem. Smiling tends to be something your body does when you're relaxed and happy and your subconscious brain is in control. Smiling can help putting. Try it and see.

One way both teams and individuals can help themselves to an optimistic frame of mind is visualization. Visualization is a kind of purposeful, intense imagination. As I've recounted, I suggested it to LeBron James. Other great athletes have figured it out for themselves. Sam Snead once told me how he did this instinctively during the peak years of his golf career. He would get into bed at night after a tournament round and replay every shot in his imagination. But when his replay came to a shot he hadn't played well, he edited it. He erased the memory of the poor shot and instead visualized himself playing the shot correctly. A hooked drive into the woods became a straight drive down the fairway. A putt left short became a putt that rolled into the hole. And Sam would awake the next day feeling refreshed and optimistic.

I did something similar with the University of Virginia basketball team I worked with in 1984. That year the Cavaliers weren't expected to do much. The great Ralph Sampson had just graduated, and nobody thought the players we had left were of his caliber. We started the year 13-10, just an average team.

But slowly the team caught fire. During that season, I taught a pass/fail class to the basketball team on sports psychology. It was a genuine class. The players had to do research and write papers. We covered topics like confidence, team unity, and adjusting to playing roles within the team. Virginia, though never ranked in the top twenty-five, squeaked into the NCAA tournament and went on a roll, winning three straight games before playing a highly regarded Indiana team, with Uwe Blab and Steve Alford, in the Elite Eight.

Before that game, Coach Terry Holland and I assembled the team in a quiet, dimly lit room. I told the players to relax, close their eyes, and focus on my voice. I then described scenarios for the upcoming game. In some of them, I described Virginia hitting the floor hot and commanding the game. In others, I described Virginia staying cool under pressure and winning a close one at the buzzer. In one, I described Virginia falling behind early, staying cool, and catching up. All of the scenarios, though, ended in triumph. They were all intended to help the team feel optimistic and confident.

And they did. Virginia won 50–48 and advanced to the Final Four for the second time in school history. They then lost to a very talented Houston team, with Hakeem Olajuwon, by two points in the semifinals. Were we optimistic for Houston, too? We were. Optimism doesn't guarantee anything in sports. It just improves your chances. I liken it to the impact knowledgeable card-counting has on blackjack. If a player can count and keep track of the face cards and tens that are played, he can improve his chances of winning money. But he can't guarantee that when he pushes a big stack of chips onto the table, the dealer won't deal himself a twenty-one and beat him.

While the correlation between optimism and success is imperfect, there is an almost perfect correlation between negative thinking and failure. If you look at a golf hole before you hit a tee shot and fill your mind with worries about hitting it into woods, water, or sand, I can almost guarantee you won't hit your best drive, and you probably will indeed find woods, water, or sand.

So why wouldn't you be optimistic if it were a choice you could make?

And it is a choice. It's the choice Padraig Harrington made. It's the choice John Calipari helped Doron Lamb make. I met my friend Bob Sherman when I was consulting for Merrill Lynch and he was in charge of all the firm's offices in the eastern United States. Bob played football for Iowa and the

Pittsburgh Steelers before he entered the business world; he was an instinctive optimist. When he started trying to sell securities, it wasn't easy. Normally, in that business, only one in twenty-five sales calls results in a sale. That's pretty daunting, and it's the reason so many new financial consultants wash out of the business within a few years. Whatever optimism they had can't withstand the pain of so many rejections. Bob chose to see things differently. Every time a prospect told him no, he said to himself, "Good. I'm that much closer to the one person in twenty-five who'll say yes."

That's a classic mental strategy that's probably taught to all new salespeople. But it's classic because it works, if you believe in it.

I have had many clients who tell me that while they believe some people are by nature optimistic, they are by nature the glass-half-empty kind. My reply to that is, "Okay. Are you only going to tackle the challenges that are easy for you?"

If not, then the first thing you have to do is decide that being optimistic is important to you, because you understand that optimism is essential to fulfilling your dreams and attaining your goals. Once you make that decision, you have to start looking at things from a different perspective. To take one example, let's say that the American economy turns down and it gets tougher to succeed. Are you going to focus on all the gloom-and-doom stories in the media? Or are you going to focus on people like Bill Gates and Mark Zuckerberg, who have done rather well in a down economy? You get to choose. Will you own your mind or let others own it? Will you see yourself succeeding where others don't?

Are you going to generalize in a negative way from every setback you encounter? Suppose, to take an example, that you ask a handsome, personable guy out for a date, and he says no. Are you going to immediately and irrevocably conclude that you're just not in his league, that you never will be, and that you might as well give up on finding a tremendous guy because you're just fish bait? You could choose to think that way, but it would be disastrous for your social life.

You could also choose to think, "Well, one guy turned me down, but that doesn't have anything to do with whether the next one will. Maybe he just had something else going on in his life that made it impossible for him to date anyone. Maybe he's just not smart enough to realize what he's missing. Well, some other guy is going to luck out."

That's the way champions think after the setbacks and losses they inevitably suffer. Misfortune happens to everyone. Champions just refuse to let it push them into doubtful, fearful thinking. If they miss a fairway, they think about how good they will feel if they make birdie from the woods. If they miss a green, they think about how much they enjoy showing off their chipping, pitching, and bunker play. If they hit a mediocre bunker shot, they think about how great it would be to make a twenty-footer for par. If they have a bad round, they decide the odds will be in their favor the next time. Their optimism makes it easy for them to stay juiced, excited about their prospects and willing to work hard. It would indeed be illogical to persist if you thought you didn't have a chance to succeed.

I understand that everyone, including champions, has occasional doubts. No one should be upset if doubt occasionally enters his mind. But whether they are golfers or people in other endeavors, individuals who achieve durable, frequent success are optimists. They shake off their doubts and know in their heads and in their hearts that in the long run, they are going to be successful, they're going to have great careers, everything will fall into place, and wonderful things will happen to them—if they keep doing the right stuff.

3.

A Confident Self-Image

I F I were asked to list my role models in the field of psychology, I'd start with William James. One of the great minds of the nineteenth century, James taught for many years at Harvard and is credited with offering the first psychology course in the United States. After years of thought and research about the human mind and human behavior, James wrote this:

"People tend to become what they think about themselves."

There is enormous wisdom in that sentence. And there's enormous hope. James was wise enough to see that we are each the biggest influence on our own destiny. More importantly, he understood that we each have the power to construct our own self-image and that the self-image we construct will very likely determine what we become in life.

In my work with people striving to be exceptional, I see James's principle at work all the time. Exceptional people choose to think about themselves in ways that contribute to their success. Put another way, they choose to construct confident self-images.

Confidence and optimism are closely related, but they're different. I define optimism as a general faith that things will turn out well if an individual applies himself. Confidence is more specific. It usually applies to a particular skill or set of skills. A girl, for instance, might be very confident about her math ability but not so confident when she plays golf. If she continues to be confident in math and lack confidence in golf, I can predict that she'll be much better at math than at golf.

Most people intuitively agree with this. They understand the strong correlation between confidence and success. They've probably seen it play out in their own lives.

I've seen the evidence for the power of confidence in my work with champions. In 1989, I had a chance to talk to Ben Hogan. He won the first and only British Open he contested, at Carnoustie in 1953. You always hear about Hogan's work ethic, and it was indeed a major element in his greatness. But so was his confidence. Hogan told me, "I went to Carnoustie and told people I was there to win the tournament and that I did not plan on ever returning." And after winning the tournament, he was true to his word. The trip to Britain was just too tough on his legs, and he never went back. But for that one event, he chose not to think he'd need a few competitions to get used to links golf. He chose to think he'd win. And he did. I was particularly impressed that he chose to tell the British media about how confident he was. Today, he might be accused of talking trash. But he was just being honest.

A lot of people can understand that Hogan's confidence,

in addition to his golf skills, was critical to his success. But they'd probably say that Hogan earned his confidence by winning. Most people have trouble with the idea that an individual can choose to be confident. They think that confidence is something an individual acquires only by succeeding at something. They might agree, for instance, with the statements "A golfer needs confidence in order to win a tournament. Confidence comes from winning."

If both of those statements were true, no one would win a tournament for the first time, because how could anyone get the confidence needed to win for the first time?

I have no doubt that the easiest way for a golfer to attain a confident self-image is to experience repeated, early success by wide margins over players a few years older. That's the path Tiger Woods took, and some people think that's the only path. I can't count the number of clients I've heard tell me that they lack confidence because they didn't have the kind of early, sustained success Tiger had.

In truth, very few people have that sort of early success. Yet many people become confident. That's because a good portion of the trait we call confidence resides in the subconscious parts of the brain. Our subconscious is very susceptible to suggestion. (That's why advertising can be so effective. You may watch a pizza commercial late at night on television and your conscious brain may react by thinking, "That stuff's not good for me." But your subconscious brain is thinking, "Looks good! I'm hungry!" A short while later, you're eating.) Your subconscious monitors all the thoughts you have about yourself, and it does so uncritically. If your conscious mind thinks,

"I'm a very good salesman because people like me," your subconscious doesn't evaluate, deconstruct, or analyze. It simply records. It accommodates the input you've provided.

You can think of your self-image as an archive of all the thoughts you have ever had about yourself. However, all thoughts are not equally important. Recent thoughts are more influential than thoughts that occurred further in the past. Thoughts associated with powerful emotions are more memorable, and thus more influential, than thoughts to which you attached no emotion.

To take an example, suppose a musician played a piece perfectly a hundred times during practices and rehearsals. Then, on the evening of the premiere performance, with people who meant a lot to him listening, he made a mistake. The emotionally charged, more recent thoughts that he has about himself and that mistake are likely to be more influential than the unemotional thoughts he had during rehearsals. The musician will need to take extra care to make sure he rebuilds his self-image and confidence.

How do you do that? You understand that you are not a helpless victim of misfortune. You don't have to be a prisoner of a bad experience. You make sure you continually feed useful, positive thoughts to the subconscious. If one of my golfing clients has a problem with skulling or chunking pitch shots, I often advise him to begin keeping a notebook in which he records every good pitch shot he hit during the day, even in practice. The act of writing down a thought about a successful shot helps reinforce its importance in the subconscious registry.

But it's not necessary to write things down. The great

Jack Nicklaus showed this truth to me some years ago, when I was working with the Georgia Tech golf team, coached by my friend Puggy Blackmon. Jack's son Michael played for the Yellow Jackets that year and Jack spoke at the team's season-ending banquet. During his speech, talking about his career, he stated that he had never three-putted on the seventy-second green of a tournament. After the speech, Jack took questions from the audience. A man stood up.

"Mr. Nicklaus, with all due respect, you have three-putted on the last green of a tournament," the man said. "I remember seeing—" He was about to go on and give an example. And in fact, the man was right. But Jack cut him off.

"Sir, you're mistaken," Jack said. "I have never three-putted the last hole of a tournament or missed inside of three feet." And that was the end of that.

It wasn't that Jack was exaggerating; he certainly had no need to impress a group of people at a Georgia Tech banquet. I have no doubt that Jack sincerely believed what he said. Jack has that sort of mind. He forgets mistakes. He remembers good shots. That's one reason he was confident enough to win eighteen major championships. He refused to feed his subconscious mind with a lot of thoughts about mistakes. He understood that there's absolutely no reason to relive and remember a missed putt.

That's a champion's mind. A champion understands that it's fine to savor an experience when it's positive, to remember it, to celebrate it. When an experience is negative, he understands that he can't let himself get stuck in it. He can see no benefit from ingraining a bad experience by reliving it.

I imagine that the man who questioned Jack thought he was being helpful, trying to set the record straight. If so, he was thinking like an amateur. The champion doesn't care about keeping an accurate record in his own mind. He thinks and remembers in ways that will help him achieve and maintain a confident self-image.

After Jack left the gathering, the man in the audience approached me and asked, "What's Jack's problem? Is he in denial?"

His question irked me. "Jack came here as the greatest player in history to share with you how he thinks. He didn't come here to learn how *you* think," I said. Then I told him that Jack Nicklaus never putted until he could "make it in his mind" before he actually struck the ball. He saw every putt going in the hole. That was all he could control and, consequently, all he cared about. So from that point of view, Jack had an accurate memory of his putting history.

This ability is counterintuitive for a lot of people. We're taught in school to revisit and think about our mistakes. Our correct answers are passed over and taken for granted; the teacher puts a big, red X next to mistakes. I know many golfers who instantly forget all the good shots they hit. To them, good shots are supposed to happen, and there's nothing remarkable about them. I've worked for many years with Hall of Fame golfer Tom Kite. Tom is very demanding of himself; he tends to shrug at his good shots because he expects good shots of himself. He tends to remember his occasional poor shot and work very hard to make sure the same mistake doesn't happen again. Some of this attitude is fine, and it's one reason

Tom has been so successful. But I make it a point to remind him to take pleasure in his good shots and remember them, too. I urge him to work to be emotionally detached from his bad shots, to shrug them off. It's the opposite of what many people tend to do.

I find this counseling important to many clients. I worked with a young woman recently, a senior in high school. She was about to embark on a college golf career. I played a round with her to see the state of her game. She hit the ball far enough to be successful at the college level, but her bunker play was not up to the standards of successful college golfers. She wasn't confident in a bunker the way she was on the tee. She would need to work on it.

I didn't tell her that she could improve just by working on her confidence. To the contrary, I suggested that she block out a lot of time for bunker practice. I wanted her to work on shots from all the many different lies a player sees in the sand—upslopes, downslopes, sideslopes, and buried lies. I wanted her to seek out courses and bunkers with different sand types, from fine-grained to coarse. I wanted her to hit long bunker shots and delicate, short bunker shots that barely cleared the lip before settling by a tight pin.

She asked me a common question—how many bunker shots would she need to hit before she got good enough to think that her bunker play was a competitive asset? Just as I had told LeBron James, I told her I didn't know. I don't believe there is a magic number of repetitions that is required to become skillful and instinctive. The number varies with each golfer and in many cases it can be accelerated by things like the use of effective training aids and drills. I could only tell her that if she went about it in the right way, she would eventually get there.

By "the right way," I meant that I wanted her to work on her confidence as she worked on her physical skills. I told her I would love to see her confidence get way ahead of her actual physical skill. I wanted her to spend time every day visualizing herself hitting great bunker shots. When she practiced or played, I wanted her to enjoy her good shots, to make them more memorable, and, as Jack Nicklaus did, to forget the mistakes. That meant she had to steel herself against getting upset when she hit an unsatisfactory bunker shot.

In short, I asked her to make a commitment to all the things that would help rebuild her self-image as a bunker player. When she thought about her bunker play, she was to think about her good shots. When she visualized, she was to visualize good shots. When she talked about her bunker play, I wanted her to be talking about how her skills were improving and she felt really good about the way things were going. The subconscious brain listens to what we say to others as well as ourselves. I wanted her to work on enjoying her good shots and remembering them, while attaching no emotion to bad shots and quickly forgetting them.

Some people tell me that making this change in the way they think is hard work. I agree. But so is training the body. If an individual wants to be exceptional, it's part of the challenge. Thinking correctly will separate that individual from the average person.

To some clients, this process is counterintuitive because

they don't understand the subconscious and how it works. They find it hard to believe that a part of their mind is so trusting and susceptible to suggestion. But it is. Remember that the subconscious brain is the best controller of many activities, particularly motor skills. It's the part of the brain that does best at directing golf swings and violin performances. It's also a part of the brain that is engaged in whatever we do, even if we try to maintain control with our conscious brains. At the moment of truth, your subconscious had better be saying, "Oh, yeah. I got this. No problem," rather than saying, "Uh-oh. Trouble. Time to panic."

I have players who tell me, "That's all fine, doc, but I've just missed four cuts in a row, and there's nothing good I can give my subconscious." I could hear the same sort of protest from a person who's just mailed out one hundred résumés without getting a job or from someone whose store is going into the red during a recession.

I counsel golfers that the key question in this sort of stressful situation is how they perceive what's happening to them. Yes, they've missed some cuts. But do they jump from there to the general conclusion that they can't play golf well? Or do they perceive events in a different, constructive way? The truth is that there's a very fine line sometimes between missing the cut and finishing in the top twenty-five. It might be one or two putts a round that the player missed. And it might be that on one or two putts a round, the player allowed doubt to enter his mind as he struck the ball. So what the player could conclude from recent events is "I'm hitting the ball well enough to make cuts and make money, but I need to rededicate myself to my putting routine and make sure my mind is where it needs to be for every putt."

Golfers get into real trouble when they allow themselves to become so emotional after a skein of setbacks that they exaggerate their mistakes and ignore what they've done well. They can launch themselves into a downward spiral that destroys their self-image and their confidence.

Our culture has a fundamental ambivalence about confidence. Yes, we recognize that it's important. But I also sense in some parents and coaches a belief that they don't want their children or their players to be *too* confident. If you listen to the pro football preview shows on television, you'll always hear that one or two games this week are "trap" games, so called because the more talented team is thought to be too confident and therefore ripe for an upset. Some coaches talk a lot about players being overconfident. I think they're misguided.

Champions understand that they must be confident to a point that some people might find offensive. The smart ones don't want to feel this way or act this way in their routine, noncompetitive interactions with other people. But once they step onto the court or inside the ropes at a golf tournament, they do. Rory McIlroy, for instance, is a personable, modest young man at the dinner table and in the locker room. But he's learned not to feel that way in tournament competitions. "I just try and have a bit of an attitude, you know?" he said recently. "I needed to be a little more cocky, a little more arrogant on the golf course—but just on the golf course."

I think back to coaches like John Wooden and Vince

Lombardi. Neither Wooden, coaching the UCLA Bruins in basketball, nor Lombardi, coaching the Green Bay Packers of the National Football League, ever worried too much about his opponents. Wooden never even scouted the opposition. Both men told their players that if they played their games, executed their plays, they would win. If they didn't win, it didn't mean they were inferior. It just meant that they ran out of time. That was confidence.

I can't think of a golf tournament I've ever seen lost because a player was too confident. Sometimes, a player will ask me if he should worry about being overconfident. I'll ask him to tell me the last time he missed a putt or hit a drive into the woods because he was overconfident. No one has ever given me an example. But when I ask if they've ever missed a putt or a drive because they lacked confidence, the answer is always yes.

To be clear, when I speak of confidence, I exclude both arrogance and laziness. To me, confidence doesn't mean that an individual or a team fails to prepare. Though they were supremely confident, neither Lombardi's nor Wooden's teams ever stinted on preparation. Their coaches wouldn't let them. Lombardi's players quickly learned that they had to be in place for practices and meetings ten minutes before the scheduled starting time. They called it "Lombardi time." Wooden and Lombardi both worked their teams hard and got them into excellent physical condition. Lombardi preached that "fatigue makes cowards of us all," and I know Wooden believed in that as well. They emphasized fundamentals and drilled their teams on them over and over again. They paid attention to detail. Wooden even started each season by teaching his players how he wanted them to wear their socks and tie the laces on their sneakers. All of that preparation and dedication is, to my mind, intertwined with confidence.

I can't see how people could get lazy if they were confident. If you were confident and thought you could do anything you put your mind to, I would think you'd be highly dedicated and committed to whatever it was you wanted to do. By the same token, I think it would be very unlikely for someone to be committed and dedicated if he wasn't confident. Why would someone work hard if he didn't think he could succeed?

Confidence is essential to patient, sustained effort, and patient, sustained effort is what leads to success. Confidence buoys athletes during the inevitable slumps. I remember one year sitting with golfer Tim Simpson and baseball player Mike Schmidt. Tim had gotten off to a bad start and was worried. He asked Mike what he did if he experienced an early-season slump.

"Well, I'm a three hundred hitter and I always wind up with about one hundred RBIs and thirtysomething home runs," Mike said. "All I know is if I'm batting one sixty at the All-Star break, I'm going to have a great second half." That's the way a confident player thinks.

Confidence is not, unfortunately, something you own forever once you've found it. It's something you must constantly work on.

Some years ago, I had a conversation about confidence with the wife of a young golfer I was counseling.

"Dr. Rotella," she said, "when I met my husband, we were in college and he was one of the most confident people I had ever met. It's part of the reason I was attracted to him and fell in love with him. Now he has to pay you to work on his confidence. Why is that?"

It was a good question, and I thought about it for a while.

"Would you say that a lot of the wives of players on the Tour are good-looking?" I asked.

"Definitely," she said. Most people would agree with her.

"And would you say they're confident about their looks?" I asked.

She nodded. "I think so."

"Well, what do you think would happen to them if you put them to work as receptionists at the Eileen Ford Modeling Agency for a few months?" I asked. "How would they feel about themselves if they had to spend eight hours a day answering phones in a room filled with the most beautiful women in the world?"

She nodded. "I see your point."

Most successful people go through something like the hypothetical experience I suggested to my client's wife. In the case of golfers on the PGA Tour, most of them were far and away the best junior golfers in their clubs or their hometowns. In college, they were generally the top players on their teams. Every time they went to practice, their confidence was reinforced because they hit the ball longer and straighter than anyone else on the practice tee. But then they turn pro, and they make it to the PGA Tour. They realize that everyone they see on the practice tee hits it long and straight. Some of them hit it longer and straighter than they do. It's a shock to a lot of players, and their confidence can falter.

I've seen the same thing happen to good college basketball players who make it to the NBA but don't immediately become stars. In college, they were the go-to guys. They were the ones who took the last shots, the ones who had the ball in the final seconds, because they were the ones their coaches wanted on the line for critical free throws. But in the NBA, maybe someone else is the star and someone else takes the critical shots and goes to the line in the final moments. Maybe the coach decides they have limitations of speed, size, or something else and puts them on the bench. Their confidence can falter.

You might say, "Well, their confidence *should* be different because they've moved up a level and the players are bigger, faster, and more skilled."

Perhaps. There's no question that the players in the NBA are bigger and faster than the players in college basketball. It may be that against this tougher physical competition, a good college player's scoring and defense will decline. But in pro ball, the free-throw line is still fifteen feet from the basket and the basket is still ten feet from the floor. There should be no reason why a player who was a confident 80 percent free-throw shooter in college should deteriorate in the pros. Yet I've seen it happen many times. The guy who knocked down the game winner time after time in college becomes an NBA bench player and shoots bricks on the rare occasions when he takes a free throw in the final seconds of a game. It's not because he doesn't practice free throws enough. Professionals have no schoolwork to impinge on their practice time and the ones I've worked with are diligent about their practice routines.

It's simply that their confidence has slipped. In many of the cases I have worked with, it's apparent that the player never learned to develop confidence within himself. He was dependent on his coaches in high school and college to do it for him. His coaches believed in him. His coaches praised him. The player's subconscious mind internalized all that reinforcement, and he was confident. In the pros, it became evident that the coach believed in other players more. So the player's confidence in himself evaporated.

Sometimes I work with golfers who believe they'll attain confidence when they perfect their golf swings. That's a damaging illusion. In the first place, no one ever perfects the golf swing. On top of that, you don't have to be perfect to be confident. The two best golfers of the last twenty years, Tiger Woods and Phil Mickelson, have never learned to drive the ball consistently straight. They both miss a lot of fairways. In their heydays, they compensated for it. They never confused the ability to drive the ball straight with the ability to get the ball in the hole. Tiger might spend almost an entire tournament relying on irons off the tee. Phil changed the mix of clubs in his bag. If they weren't able to hit fairways with their drivers in a given week, they were confident that they could find a way to win without that element of the game. And if they got on a hot streak with their drivers, their confidence just grew.

Let me be clear. Regardless of the club in their hands, Tiger and Phil are highly skilled. And skill is a part of the equation when we're talking about confidence. But they don't need to be perfectly skilled to have confident self-images and to believe they can win. Neither does anyone else.

I have clients, though, who still spend their careers chasing perfect skills rather than building a confident self-image. They're never satisfied with their games. Maybe they feel that they need to add ten yards to their tee shots, or straighten them out, or learn to draw the ball or fade the ball. So they find a coach who works with them on that. And their tee shots improve. Then they decide that their putting is holding them back. So they find a putting coach who works with them on their stroke. And they keep at that until they're rolling the ball perfectly. Then they decide their short game needs work, and they go on a campaign to improve their pitch shots. And when they've done that, they decide their driver has been letting them down and they go back to work breaking their long game down.

That's not the way to build confidence. It's not the way a champion thinks.

Take the 2014 U.S. Open champion, Martin Kaymer. I haven't worked with Martin, but he's a candid interview, and he's disclosed a lot about his thinking. He won the PGA Championship in 2010 and ascended to the number one position in the world rankings early in 2011. Then he succumbed to the temptation to try to perfect his skills. He decided that his natural fade off the tee wasn't good enough and set about learning how to draw the ball. As a result, he had two seasons that were, by his standards, unsuccessful.

For whatever reason, though, he decided in 2014 that he was confident he could win. It definitely wasn't because his golf game was finally perfect. That was evident at Pinehurst No. 2. Time and again, Kaymer would miss a green and face a situation that called for a delicate, precise chip shot or low pitch off a tight lie to one of the course's convex putting surfaces. But he didn't chip or pitch the ball. He putted the ball through swales and up banks toward the flag—the sort of choice that amateurs make when they lack confidence in their short games. At one point in the final round, rather than hit a pitch over a bunker, he putted around the bunker to the green and took his chances with a twenty-five-foot par putt. It was evident that his short game was less than perfect. But that didn't stop Kaymer from believing in himself and running away with the tournament. He just kept looking for a way to win with what he had.

He was hardly the first successful golfer to think this way. Again, I think of Ben Hogan. Hogan, as almost all students of golf know, worked very hard on perfecting his golf swing. But fewer golfers know that he only started to win regularly when he stopped worrying so much about that swing. "In 1946, my attitude suddenly changed," he once wrote. "I honestly began to feel that I could play fairly well each time I went out, that there was no practical reason for me to feel that I might suddenly lose it all. I guess that what lay behind my new confidence was this: I had stopped trying to do a great many things perfectly because it had become clear in my mind that this ambitious over-thoroughness, my perfectionism, was neither possible, nor advisable, nor even necessary. All you needed to groove were the fundamental movements, and there weren't so many of them. . . . My shot-making started to take on a new and more stable consistency."

I've read that passage to a lot of players who revere Hogan's memory and consider him a model for hard work. Almost invariably, they say that while they've read and reread everything Hogan ever published about the golf game, they don't remember that passage. I tell them that's because when they read Hogan's book, they were looking for a way to perfect their golf swings. They weren't looking for Hogan's suggestion that there was a time to decide that their swings were good enough and to go out and play confident golf.

I see evidence of this principle in nearly every human endeavor, not just golf. In Virginia, there's a special, selective school in Fairfax County, the Thomas Jefferson High School for Science and Technology. Admission is very competitive, and 66 percent of the incoming freshman class in 2014 was of Asian descent, a number far higher than the Asian share of the population. Now, I'm sure that the biggest reason for this rate of success by Asian students is that they work very hard at mastering math and science, just as Ben Hogan worked very hard at mastering the golf swing. But I am equally certain that the Asian students have a high degree of confidence in their math and science abilities. This confidence may come from their parents. It may come from seeing lots of older Asian students do well in those subjects. But they have it. When they encounter a tough problem or a tough course, they plug away at it. They persevere. Their confidence makes a major contribution to their success. As William James would have predicted, they become what they think about themselves. They think they're good at math and science, so they are. Their confidence reinforces the virtues of working hard and getting better, which leads to people telling them how gifted they are, which leads to more confidence.

Conversely, I've seen a lack of confidence sabotage effort. I have frequently worked with financial services companies over the years, including Morgan Stanley. Like most companies in that sector, Morgan Stanley has been emphasizing to its financial consultants the importance of attracting wealthier clients. Small accounts cost just as much as big accounts to service. A financial consultant with many small clients is usually inefficient. (For whatever reason, it seems that small clients call their financial consultants a lot more often with a lot more questions than big clients do.) If Morgan Stanley is going to improve its performance, its financial consultants have to improve their performance by seeking and landing clients with major amounts of money to invest.

This is a tough challenge for many financial consultants, and the challenge starts with their confidence. They certainly understand the logic of going after big accounts, and they generally agree with it. But they lack confidence in their ability to sell themselves to wealthier clients. Maybe it's because they were brought up by parents who weren't themselves wealthy. Maybe they don't feel that they know enough about trusts and estate plans and other aspects of managing wealth.

Whatever the reason, some Morgan Stanley financial consultants fail this test. After a while, Morgan Stanley lets them go, and they wind up working for smaller companies that are more inclined to give a home to them and their book of middling clients.

To those who ask how they can develop the confidence to go after major accounts, my advice is similar to what I tell golfers with confidence problems. It's a two-pronged approach. Work on needed skills. Work on confidence. But don't make a confident self-image dependent on perfecting skills.

They have to change the way they see people with lots of money. What is it that makes them think wealthy people won't want to associate with them, won't want to invest with them? Often, this involves rethinking their self-images. Are they really confident about their abilities as a financial consultant? Do they truly believe they can help people invest wisely and earn good returns? If they do believe this, then they have to tell themselves that anyone, no matter how wealthy, would be wise to entrust them with his investment funds. If a financial consultant doesn't believe in herself to this degree, then maybe it's appropriate to think about a career change. To succeed, she must believe that a wealthy client would be *lucky* to do business with her because no one else will be as skilled in managing the money the client worked hard to amass.

It's possible for financial consultants to take a gradual approach to this aspect of improving their business. They might, for instance, target medical students rather than established physicians, with the idea that in a few years those medical students will have substantial amounts to invest.

As with most changes involving confidence and self-image, there are practical aspects that must be addressed. A financial consultant seeking to make this change needs a strategy to identify and become acquainted with people of means. Does he need to figure out the events they attend? The charities they patronize? The clubs they belong to? At Morgan Stanley, and I suspect with most companies, there are mentors and training sessions available to help someone address these questions.

Second, they need to make sure their skills are commensurate with the goals they're setting for themselves. They have to train themselves in tax law, trusts, and other issues the clients they want are likely to care about.

Finally, I suggest they do a lot of visualization and rehearsal. I can't imagine that there's a financial services company out there that doesn't provide new financial consultants with coaches or mentors who will help them rehearse and hone their sales presentation skills. Beyond that, it's important for anyone seeking to build confidence to visualize the process over and over again.

As with athletes, when I suggest visualization to a business client, I don't mean a quick, casual daydream. I mean focused mental preparation. I generally ask clients to set aside a dedicated time—fifteen minutes or half an hour. Many of them schedule this right before they go to sleep at night. I ask them to find a room where they won't be distracted. They must turn off their phones and the television, though appropriate music can be all right depending on the individual.

For visualization to work, it must be detailed. It has to

include the sights, sounds, tactile sensations, and smells of the experience. It has to be vivid. A vivid, sensual, detailed visualization helps convince the subconscious that the experience is actually happening. If you don't believe this is possible, consider the nightmare. Nothing real is happening outside of the sleeper's mind. But when the sleeper experiencing a nightmare awakens, he generally finds that his body is exhibiting the real physical manifestations of a frightening experience. His heart is racing. He's sweating. He's breathing hard. His subconscious "believes" the dream and orders up the physical responses of extreme fear. The goal of visualization is to persuade the subconscious that the experience is actually happening.

Speaking of fear, it's important to visualize not just immediate success but adversity and setbacks. When I led the University of Virginia's basketball teams in pregame visualization exercises, I always had the players visualize falling behind and needing to catch up. That's because adversity and setbacks are inevitable in any challenging endeavor, be it winning basketball games or winning new investment clients. What's important is not avoiding adversity, but how an individual responds to it. You have to develop a mental hardiness that responds to setbacks with energy and confidence.

So the visualization process for a financial consultant might include a client brushing off the opening pitch and forcing the consultant to think of a new tack that might work better. I've seen a training film that Vince Lombardi made for an insurance company back in the 1960s. In it, Lombardi listens to the young salesman's pitch and says, "I'm sorry, but I'm not interested." At that point, the young salesman in the film meekly and politely says, "Well, all right, thanks for giving me your time," and gets up to leave. "Is that all you've got?" Lombardi asks. "You're just going to quit? Why did you give up so easily?" Lombardi's point, and the film's, was that just as you don't stop blocking and tackling if your first drive ends in a punt, you keep selling if your first effort is rebuffed.

The visualization might also include the ultimate failure of a sales effort. This is a way to deal with the salesman's fear of being rejected. By visualizing rejection and the way it makes him feel, the visualizer starts to realize that while rejection is a setback, it's not a disaster. He can pick himself up and try again. I've seen fear of rejection paralyze financial consultants, so using visualization to realize that it's not a terminal illness can help.

And the visualization exercises will of course include successful efforts. The idea is for an individual to see herself succeeding in high-stress, high-stakes situations.

This technique works. I remember talking to the late Seve Ballesteros after he won his first Masters. He told me he had listened to a tape made by a friend for months prior to the tournament, particularly on his flight to the United States. The tape was a fictional broadcast by a reporter describing how Seve won the tournament. He listened to it, closed his eyes, and visualized it. He did it over and over. His subconscious believed in it. He told me he got to the golf course Thursday already sure he would win the Masters.

There was only one problem, he told me, his eyes twinkling a little.

"When I actually walked up the eighteenth fairway with the tournament won, I didn't feel excited and happy because I had already celebrated winning," he said. "I knew I would win when I teed it up Thursday morning."

"That's all right, Seve," I replied. "I can teach you how to party."

In his prime, Seve had a certain swagger that I see frequently in people who are exceptional. Some of them learn to hide what they really think about themselves. Some don't. Joe Namath, the Hall of Fame quarterback for the New York Jets, wrote an autobiography with the title *I Can't Wait Until Tomorrow . . . 'Cause I Get Better-Looking Every Day*. I liked that title. A lot of people didn't like Namath's personality, but to me, he was just being honest about the way he felt. In the entertainment field, Madonna has a Namath-like personality. When I see her perform, I see that the dancers behind her can dance better than she can. Some of her backup singers can sing better than she can. But she thinks she's the greatest singer and dancer on the planet, which is a big reason that she has been an enduring star.

I've talked with other champions who have almost a dual personality. Deion Sanders, off the field, struck me as a modest, helpful person, the sort of man who's involved as a Big Brother to less fortunate boys. But on the field, he became Prime Time Sanders, ready to take on any receiver in football, shut him down, and brag about it. I saw an interview with Beyoncé Knowles in which she revealed the same kind of dual persona. In her private life, she said, she is fairly shy and introverted. She likes staying home and reading or watching a movie. But on the night of a show, she transforms herself. An hour and a half before the show begins, she turns into a diva. She feels like she owns the world. She wants everyone around her to treat her like a diva. Only by feeling that way can she put on the sort of show her fans have paid to see.

Seal, the singer, has that sort of dual persona—at least, he does now. He originally came to see me because he suffered from stage fright. His career, while quite successful, was not working as well as he wanted. He'd had a big opportunity when the producer of *Batman Forever* asked to use his song "Kiss from a Rose" in the film. It became a big hit, and Seal was asked to sing it at the Grammy awards and on *The Tonight Show*. The performances did not go well. He was stiff. His throat got tight and made his voice sound constricted.

Seal got another chance; he was booked to perform at a Wembley Stadium concert on a bill with Rod Stewart and Toni Braxton. He was going to sing "Kiss from a Rose" and cover six songs by other composers. The prospect made him uncomfortable.

"Rod Stewart?" I said. "That skinny little wrinkled guy? He's the one that's going to be intimidated, being onstage with you."

"That's not how I'm looking at it," Seal said.

"Well, you're here so we can develop a different way of looking at it," I said. I told him if he went onstage feeling full of himself and refusing to be intimidated by Rod Stewart, I'd take over the job of singing duets with Toni Braxton. (I was, of course, joking.) Seal smiled and said no, thank you, he'd prefer to take care of singing with Toni himself.

We went on from there, talking about attitude and stage presence. We talked about feeling like everyone in Wembley Stadium would be there because they loved Seal and wanted him to show off his talent for them.

"I can see myself that way doing my song," Seal said. "But I've never sung the other six songs before. If you want to know the truth, I'm afraid of forgetting the words."

My dad was a big jazz fan, and he particularly loved Louis Armstrong. So did I.

"Great jazz musicians ad-lib," I said. "Louis Armstrong just started making up nonsense words if he had to, but he kept on singing, and people loved him. So if you start forgetting words, put a big, cocky smile on your face and make up nonsense. No one will know the difference."

Seal looked doubtful.

"When you were a kid, did you ever go to concerts at Wembley Stadium?" I asked him.

"Oh, yeah." He smiled.

"Did you ever go to see one of your favorite singers and your goal was to catch him forgetting lyrics?"

"No, I guess I didn't."

"I don't think anyone's going to be there to catch you, either."

That idea clicked with Seal, and he started to envision himself singing successfully onstage. It became easy, even pleasant for him. The last time I saw him onstage, it was hard to believe how animated and relaxed he was. He's done a wonderful job of transforming his self-image, of giving himself confidence.

When it's time for you to perform and produce, you have two choices. You can feel confident. Or, more likely, you can fail. Much of what we do in life is a little bit like a comedian going onstage to do a stand-up routine. If the comedian doesn't have confidence in his material and himself, doesn't believe that it's funny and that he's talented, his jokes, no matter how brilliant, are going to fall flat. No one will laugh. He'll be worried too much about what the audience will think. No one performs well in a state of doubt and fear.

I don't care if a person's job is something that seems, at first glance, to demand doubt and fear. If an engineer is tasked with designing and building a bridge, of course at some point early in the process, he needs to make certain that the design, steel, and concrete are of the right quality. But to build a superior bridge, I want him to feel that his project is going to be the best bridge anyone's ever built. It's going to be safe, effective, and beautiful, and it's going to last forever. If he doesn't feel that way, his design and engineering talents will be stifled, and the project will be a dreary mediocrity.

Some of my clients have a hard time envisioning themselves with this much confidence. If they're golfers, I sometimes suggest to them that they imagine that God appeared to them and said, "You're going to have a great career. You're going to win dozens of tournaments. You're going to win several major championships. Don't worry about it. You just keep working hard on your game. I've taken care of the results." And then imagine that the vision ended before the golfer could ask God which tournaments he would win and when he would win them.

He'd play from that time on with tremendous confidence. He wouldn't know exactly when his wins would come, or where. But he'd know that if he just kept doing the things he was supposed to do, the results were guaranteed. He'd step onto the first tee every Thursday thinking, "Oh, boy! I can't wait to find out if this is going to be one of my weeks."

If you want to transform your life, if you want to grow, you have to change the way you see yourself and the way you respond to the world around you—just as surely as you would if God appeared to you and told you everything was set.

The truth is that you don't need to wait for divine intervention to have that sort of confidence. The miracle has already happened, in the creation of the human brain. You need to take responsibility for using it and give confidence to yourself.

4.

Respecting Your Talent

LEARNED EARLY in my career that no one can weigh or measure talent. I was working as a coach with the University of Connecticut's lacrosse team while I finished my PhD. I was young, energetic, and enthusiastic, and I believed I could see talent in players that others couldn't see. I also believed I could discern the absence of talent. We had a player I will simply call Larry, and he was perhaps the slowest lacrosse player I had ever seen. Slower than death. Nothing about him was impressive. I just couldn't see any talent in Larry, and I found ways to make sure he didn't play much.

After that season, I finished my degree and began teaching at the University of Virginia. I was startled the next spring when the news came down to me from UConn that Larry had broken the school season scoring record. I called a coach in Connecticut to make sure I had heard correctly. Yes, he said. It turned out that Larry was slow of foot, but he had quick hands. So the year after I left, UConn stationed him at crease attack, where he didn't have to move too much and looked so unimpressive (UConn opponents being no better judges of talent than I had been) that no one guarded him very closely. They double-teamed someone else, and Larry was often open right in front of the opposition net. He'd get a pass and use those quick hands to flick the ball into the goal.

I said to myself, "Rotella, don't ever think you know what talent looks like. You don't." And I've tried since then never to judge an athlete's talent, certainly not based on the sort of superficial criteria that are often all we can really know about another individual at first glance.

That lesson was reinforced some years later when I worked with Greg Maddux of the Chicago Cubs. As a young pitcher, Greg didn't fit many scouts' template of a talented prospect. Coming out of high school, he wasn't recruited by any major colleges, and every major-league team passed on him in the first round of the draft. That's because Greg wasn't especially tall and he couldn't throw the ball especially hard. As a youngster, he could get his fastball over ninety miles per hour on occasion, but just barely. (In his prime, his fastball usually topped out in the high eighties.) Most scouts are predisposed to think that pitching talent begins at around ninety-five miles per hour. They salivate over a kid who can touch one hundred miles per hour.

Greg chose not to believe in their evaluations. He decided that real pitching talent consisted of being able to change speeds, analyze hitters' weaknesses, and locate the ball precisely at the edges (or, sometimes, just outside the edges) of the strike zone. He could do those things, and he worked very hard to improve his control and consistency. Without a big fastball, he became the best pitcher I've ever seen and, I would submit, perhaps the best pitcher baseball has ever seen. He was of course a first-ballot Hall of Fame selection. A lot of youngsters in his situation would have paid attention to the opinions of scouts who watched them in high school and chosen another line of work. Greg Maddux chose to believe in his talent. He found a way to be great by focusing on what he could do rather than using his limitations as an excuse for failing.

The question of talent arises frequently when I counsel golfers. They generally don't come to me because they're brimming with confidence, because they've been hanging on to leads on Sunday, or because they feel that they play their best golf when the stakes are highest. Quite the opposite. My clients tend to be players who, while they may have been quite successful by others' standards, have disappointed themselves. They're not getting the results they want, and they sense that the way they think is part of their problem.

As we discuss things, I often hear, early in the conversation, something like, "Doc, I've got to develop a great mental game, because I don't have _____'s talent."

You can fill in the blank with names like Greg Norman, Tiger Woods, and Rory McIlroy. If I'd worked in the 1960s, I'm sure that Arnold Palmer and Jack Nicklaus's names would have been occupying the blank. Golf usually has an alpha dog, and most people think that guy is the alpha dog because of some mysterious God-given gift we label "talent." And just as certainly as they think that Jack or Greg or Tiger got a disproportionate share when God handed out talent, they feel that they themselves got slighted.

It's worth noting here that the alpha dog of any given period is usually a player who hits it a long way. People in golf continually confuse length off the tee with talent, just as baseball scouts often confuse velocity with talent. They don't know the difference between a long-drive competition and a game won by taking the fewest strokes getting the ball into a hole. Of course, it's better to hit it long than hit it short, assuming you're reasonably accurate. But there are thousands of long-ball hitters out there who can't play for a Division I college team. There are dozens of long-driving contests won by players who can't score well enough to make a living on the Hooters Tour. Each year, the top tiers of the PGA Tour's money list include many players who are nowhere near the top in driving distance. And the long hitters who do lead the money list, like Rory McIlroy and Tiger Woods, generally do so not just because of how long they hit the ball, but because they have polished all-around games, particularly near and on the greens.

They get there not by dint of superhuman talent and length off the tee, but through hard work and superior mental qualities. Greg Norman once told me about his youth in Australia. There was a popular song at the time with the lyric "Keep on singing, don't stop singing. You're gonna be a star someday." Greg adapted it to "keep on swinging, don't stop swinging, you're going to be a star someday." He played that song in his mind for hour after hour of practice. He sang it under his breath over a decade in which he averaged about 500 practice shots a day. He was conditioning his mind and feeding his self-confidence as he trained his swing. That's why he got so good. Jack Nicklaus was the longest hitter of his day and the alpha dog. But John Cook once told me about a Jack Nicklaus appearance before the golf team at Ohio State, their alma mater. Jack told the golf team, which included John Cook, "You have to be a legend in your own mind before you can be a legend in your own time." He was saying that confidence and a belief in your own ability are essential to being great. Not length off the tee.

Yet, the myth persists that length and talent are one and the same.

It makes me pine for the time when Ben Hogan was the dominant figure in golf. Among Hogan's many distinctions was this: almost no one thought of him as supremely talented. He was respected for the hard work he put into his game. But in Hogan's time, most people thought of Sam Snead as the player best endowed with what people generally think of as talent. Only now, when both have passed on, is it possible to say that Hogan was more talented than Snead.

That's because, looking back on their careers, it's apparent that while Snead had great gifts, including a great mind, and was a great player, Hogan surpassed him in some critical measures. Put crudely, Snead may have had more talent than Hogan from the neck down. But Hogan was a bit better from the neck up. He had the edge in tenacity, in determination, in sheer will. His mind made him, by a small but significant margin, the better player.

And yet, players still assess their own talent and the talent of their peers and rivals by much the same metrics that made Snead seem more talented than Hogan.

I can't say that I know precisely what Hogan's talent was, much less how to measure it. I can tell you that in golf, talent has almost nothing to do with a player's size or physical strength. It's only tenuously related to things like the distance a player hits the ball off the tee. I can tell you that you'll probably never see a picture accurately labeled "talent" because talent exists largely inside people.

That's why I've been delighted to see Jordan Spieth emerge in the last year as the best young American golfer. Jordan is a little bit like Hogan, and it's not just because they're both Texans. If you stood behind him and a dozen other young stars on the practice range and you didn't know who he was, you'd probably not select him as the best of the bunch, the way a generation ago, you might have seen the obvious fact that Tiger Woods hit the ball farther than anyone else and picked him as the best of the bunch. Jordan's distance off the tee is only average. But he's a great putter and he's developing an excellent mental game.

In the late autumn of 2014, he won the Australian Open, shooting 63 on the final day. Then he ran away with Tiger's Hero World Challenge. When he was interviewed after that tournament, Jordan didn't talk about his swing very much. He talked about his attitude. He said he'd learned to be more patient, to be indifferent to what his competitors were doing, to zero in on a small target, and let his swing happen. He didn't fall into the trap of thinking much about where he stood in the tournament and trying to force things. I was particularly impressed by what he said he learned by playing with Bubba Watson in the last round of the 2014 Masters, which Bubba won. A lot of players would have been impressed by Bubba's length off the tee or his ability to shape shots. Jordan took away an impression of how casual and unflappable Bubba seemed, even in the cauldron of Sunday at Augusta.

I think it would be good for American golf if Jordan's compatriots listened to what he said and realized that it's usually mental qualities that separate champions from mere big hitters. They should, because although genes play a big role in determining how far a player can hit the ball, genes don't have much to do with how he thinks. If the next alpha male in American golf is a player whose most obvious strength is his mind, I suspect it will eventually help tip the balance in the Ryder Cup back toward the American side of the Atlantic.

Let me be clear here. I am not denying the existence of physical ability. Quickness exists. Reflexes exist. Size exists. But I can also say that it's possible to overestimate their importance. I've seen athletes with great physical gifts have mediocre careers precisely because they assumed their talent would carry them and never applied themselves to getting better. Within a relatively short time, athletes with lesser physical gifts passed them by.

What I've realized over the years is the obvious—that physical talent and character are both important. I've seen that when I've observed great coaches. When I was young, growing up in Vermont, I revered Red Auerbach of the Boston Celtics. I understood that the cornerstone of Auerbach's success and the Celtics dynasty was his insistence on building his roster with players of both physical ability and character. If you didn't have character, Red wasn't going to have you. The best college basketball coaches I see today start off looking for the most physically talented high school players in the country. Then they use character as a filter. They will, for instance, stop recruiting players who aren't respectful of their parents, grandparents, and coaches. Tony Bennett, who has done a tremendous job rebuilding the University of Virginia's basketball program—the Cavaliers won the Atlantic Coast Conference regular season and tournament in 2014—often looks for players from Christian schools, because he wants the values taught in such schools in his program. Neither Tony nor anyone else wants players who lack physical abilities, because they know it's hard to out-coach a rival whose team has much greater physical talent. But Tony isn't interested in players with great physical ability who don't want to work hard, don't want to play defense, don't want to put the team's success before their individual statistics, don't want to study, and don't know how to behave themselves off the court. He understands that it's very hard to change bad character unless the player himself wants to change it.

My experience tells me that one of the best character traits for achieving exceptional results is a belief in your own talent. It's not always easy to maintain this belief. The world has a way of conveying negative opinions about people. Think about grades in school, or job applications unanswered, or any of a myriad of rejections that come to anyone. It's all too easy to react to these by thinking, "I must not be talented enough."

I see this in college athletics. Athletes at all but a handful of schools have to reckon with things that tell them, "You are not an elite talent." There are coaches and schools that didn't recruit them. There are divisions between schools, like Division I, Division II, and Division III. There are polls in the newspapers.

In the fall of 2005, I saw one such poll when I was going to George Mason University in Fairfax, Virginia, to talk to the basketball team coached by Jim Larrañaga. Jim and I had been friends for decades, ever since his days as an assistant to Terry Holland at the University of Virginia. After I parked near the Patriot Center on the GMU campus, I had some free time to think about what I was going to say. My eyes fell on a copy of *USA Today* that contained the newspaper's preseason basketball poll. Predictably enough, the poll didn't rank George Mason. Poll voters tend to vote for reputations, and they're influenced by factors like a program's history and whether it belongs to a "power conference." George Mason didn't rate highly on either count.

I decided to use that in my talk. When the team assembled, I waved the paper in front of their faces. "You're not ranked," I said. "Isn't that the craziest thing you ever heard of? How dumb can these poll voters be? They don't know that you're going to win the national championship? How embarrassed are they going to be when you win and they didn't have you even in their top twenty-five?

"How smart is Coach Larrañaga?" I went on. "When he was recruiting, he saw talent in you that other schools didn't. How dumb are all those other coaches? If you're really smart, you'll believe in Coach Larrañaga because he believes in your talent."

The talk worked pretty well. Jim told me that the next day,

he asked the team members to write down their goals for the season. Five out of the top six players said their goal was the Final Four and the national championship. Jim said those responses affected him. He decided that the team had to conduct every practice thinking that they were national title contenders. And, sure enough, George Mason became a national title contender. The Patriots got into the NCAA Tournament in 2006 and pulled off a string of upsets, beating North Carolina, Michigan State, and UConn. They got to the Final Four, where they encountered the eventual national champion, Florida. Even though they lost that game, they were the story of the tournament, a mid-major school without a long basketball tradition that covered itself in glory and acclaim. There were a lot of factors in George Mason's success. Hard work by Jim and the players was one. The talent he had spotted in kids who weren't offered scholarships by bigger basketball schools was another. But so, I am sure, was the fact that Jim and his players chose to believe in their talent. It's all about falling in love with your talent. That makes the hard work possible.

In business, I see traits that people define as talent that are analogues of the height and power people classify as talent in basketball and golf. I have run across people who were deemed "natural salesmen," and I am certain that if you want to sell things, it's probably better to be good-looking and extroverted than homely and introverted. But I don't care if someone isn't conventionally good-looking or able to crack jokes in any circumstance. That's not what makes a salesman.

Whatever the endeavor, I've come to the conclusion that the most successful people have some of what we call natural talent, but not so much that it makes them complacent. They're brimming over with the character traits, like Ben Hogan's, that promote patient, persistent, hard work. Their physical talents are sufficient to persuade them that they can be as successful as they want to be, but only if they work very hard and work very smart.

So when a golfer, or anyone else, comes to me and says, "I wish I had _____'s talent," the first thing I have to do is persuade him to change that attitude. I start by reminding him that the part of talent we see at first glance—like foot speed or size—is only part of the conglomeration of traits we call talent. Most of those traits are more difficult to observe and measure than an individual's time for forty yards or his maximum bench press. We know that some of the most important traits, the character traits, are internal, and that we can influence them in ourselves. Perseverance, for example, is an essential component of any exceptional person's talent. And anyone can persevere if he wants to badly enough. When I counsel players, I continually stress the importance of loving their own talents. You can't tell me you have a great attitude if you don't love your own abilities.

Golfers I work with frequently ask me what I think their potential is. If they're new clients, I answer, truthfully, that I don't know. When I begin working with someone, I can gauge fairly quickly the degree to which he's developed physical skills. But it takes a lot longer to learn about the player's mind and the personal qualities that I believe are the indices of real talent.

What are these qualities?

One is a passion for the game, a passion that will sustain the player during inevitable periods of struggle and make it easier to persevere.

Two is the player's self-image and confidence. A huge part of talent is the way a player sees himself, even if he's not yet been successful. Is he the kind of kid who has a bedrock belief that when he finally puts it all together, he'll win? If so, that's real talent.

Third, I like to see a young player whose personality makes him fun to coach and support. No one gets to the top alone. A golfer needs a good swing coach and a spouse, family, and friends who believe in him and encourage him. He may need a trainer to help with his strength and flexibility and a sports psychologist to help with his thinking. All of these helpers have to believe in him. A golfer with an upbeat personality attracts these people. They enjoy working with him and being around him. He's the sort of pupil who lets his teacher know that he believes in what the teacher is suggesting and he'll work at it until he gets it. He's the sort of person who never blames his failures on others, who puts a bad round behind him as soon as he leaves the golf course. No matter the level and ranking he attains, he doesn't think he's better than anyone else. He appreciates the contributions others make to his success. That, too, is real talent.

Fourth, a player needs the wisdom to pick a teacher who believes in him and to believe in that teacher. You can't develop as a player if you're constantly listening to many differing voices about how to swing and how to think. You're not likely to develop as a player if your teacher doesn't believe you can do it. So a part of real talent is the ability to select the right counselors and tune everyone else out. When he finds that teacher or teachers, the player makes it a point to show up on time for every lesson, warmed up and ready to work. That, too, is a talent. You can have all the physical tools in the world, but you can waste them if you can't distinguish good people from charlatans and parasites.

When a business client asks me for help in identifying prospective employees with real talent, I begin with some very similar criteria. In fact, I often advise businesses that recruit new college graduates to look among students who participated in sports. I tell them to seek out players who walked onto their college football or basketball teams (i.e., they were not recruited and did not have scholarships) or who played the so-called minor sports. I tell them to talk to these kids' coaches.

I tell them to recruit kids whose coaches report that they had tremendous work ethics. They lifted weights on their own during the off-season. They showed up early for practice, stayed late, and asked for extra help on their skills. They were leaders who helped push everyone on the team to work harder. And they displayed these traits both when the team did well and when it struggled through adversity. It's relatively easy to be enthused and hardworking on a team that's winning. It shows more character to display those same attributes on a team that's losing. It speaks to a person's mental toughness, toughness that will be invaluable in dealing with the setbacks and rejections that inevitably come along in a business career.

I'm not, of course, the only one who looks for these kinds

of personal traits and considers them essential to talent. I see that out in Silicon Valley, Google is indeed looking for talented software engineers. But more than mere expertise, Google prizes qualities like the ability to work with a team and lead it, to acknowledge failure and learn from it.

All of these traits of real talent have little or nothing to do with genetic inheritance, with the ability to run fast, jump high, get a perfect score on the math SAT, or hit a golf ball over the fence at the end of the range. They are all traits a person can decide to cultivate within himself.

So why would you say that you wish you had someone else's talent?

In many cases, clients say this because it's a convenient excuse for giving up on themselves. If you decide you don't have Tiger Woods's talent, it makes it so much more justifiable to settle for mediocrity. Why work hard at your game when your lack of talent will forever hold you back? If you do get into contention in a tournament and you fail to play well on Sunday, it's not because you didn't get your mind where it needed to be for the final round. It's because after playing over your head for a few days, you came down to earth and finished back where people with your talent level belong. Or so goes the rationalization.

Sometimes players do this because they're afraid of their talent. Consciously or not, they see it as a burden. They worry that their lives will be miserable if they don't "live up to their potential." So they spend their time trying to convince themselves and others that they're not as talented as they're perceived to be.

This is true in virtually any walk of life. I'm no literary scholar, but I know that Leo Tolstoy was a giant of nineteenth-century literature and Ernest Hemingway was a giant of the next century. Hemingway was the competitive sort, and he liked boxing. He sometimes spoke, metaphorically, of getting into the ring and slugging it out with Tolstoy. That suggests the belief he had in his talent. That belief sustained his early career, when he had little or no money and no college degree. It supported his habit of reading the great writers to see what he could learn from them. It supported the hours he spent revising his writing in the belief that he could make his prose perfectly spare.

Compare this to an aspiring writer who decides he doesn't have the talent of a Tolstoy or a Hemingway. Will he spend hours revising and rewriting in the belief he can make his prose perfect? Will he have the audacity to think that he can write novels that become classics? Will he pick his own reading material with the thought that he needs to train his mind by ingesting the work of great writers?

Probably not. It's more likely, in my experience, that he'll abandon that novel before it gets done, because writing a novel is hard work, and why go through that pain if you're not really talented? He will limit himself, just as Hemingway might have limited himself to writing news articles for the *Kansas City Star* if he hadn't respected his own talent.

That's what golfers do when they decide someone else has more talent than they have. They limit themselves. Why would you do that?

I much prefer the example of players like Tom Kite. When

he was growing up in Texas, the dominant junior player was Ben Crenshaw, his peer and friend. People saw Ben play, especially on the putting green, and they marveled at how talented he was. They didn't marvel so much when they saw Tom Kite. But Tom didn't care. He respected his own talent, and he set about working very hard to develop it. He had dreams, and he wanted to see how good he could get. After four decades, both Tom and Ben have had great professional careers. They've both won nineteen times on the PGA Tour. Ben has two Masters, but Tom has a U.S. Open and a Tournament Players Championship. Tom was the Tour's leading money winner twice and has won many times on the Champions Tour. There's no reason to compare them except that they grew up in the same town, but if I had to say whose career was better, I'd give the edge to Tom.

Tom could have said, "I must not be very talented. There's even a kid in my own hometown who's more talented than I am. I guess I'll settle for playing two-dollar Nassaus with my buddies on weekends and be happy if I can break eighty." But he didn't.

A golfer who seeks to be exceptional and respects his own talent doesn't transform rivals into giants by having an exaggerated respect for their talent while denigrating his own. I like the way Hal Sutton put it after the 2000 Players Championship, which he won in a duel with Tiger Woods. This was at a time when it seemed to many players that Tiger's talent surpassed not just their own but everyone's. When Tiger was in the field, they felt they had to play perfect golf to beat him. Trying to play perfectly isn't conducive to good golf. Consequently, Tiger won a lot of events when the players around him turned in uncharacteristically poor performances. Hal didn't do that, shooting a one-under 71 to beat Tiger by a stroke.

"When I knelt down to say my prayers last night, I didn't say them to Tiger," Hal said. "So I guess he's not God."

Hal chose to respect his own talent that day rather than Tiger's. It's one of the choices champions always make.

5.

Commitment, Perseverance, and Habit

I N MY work with businesses, I often find a pattern in the results of both a company and the individuals who work there. The numbers are good in the first quarter and good in the fourth quarter. But in the middle two quarters of the year, they decline. That's because the individuals in the company often start the year with good intentions. They work harder for a couple or three months. But they don't maintain that level of effort. They slack off. Then, in the final quarter of the year, they realize they're headed for an annual review that will not be pleasant, that might even end in termination. So they rouse themselves, work harder for a couple or three months, and finish the year with results that are not what they wanted in January but are good enough to make the annual review bearable.

This pattern will be apparent to anyone who ever noticed that his gym gets crowded in January, filled with people who disappear by April. People make commitments at the beginning of a new year, commitments to get fit, sell more, or work on their short games. But commitments are easier to make than to keep. Perseverance is a virtue in short supply.

Except, that is, among people who achieve excellence, people who live exceptional lives. I think of Paul Runyan, whom I got to know back in the 1980s, when we both worked for *Golf Digest*'s schools. Paul was a man who believed in his talent and kept his commitments. He believed in his talent enough to win the 1938 PGA Championship by beating Sam Snead in the finals 8 and 7, even though Snead hit the ball sixty or seventy yards longer than Paul did off the tee. (Paul was only five feet seven inches and he weighed maybe one hundred thirty pounds after a big meal and dessert.) Paul was the leading money winner on the PGA Tour a couple of times in the 1930s, but his playing career was cut short by World War II, when he served in the navy. After the war, he devoted himself to teaching golf with the same excellence he'd had when he played competitively, though he never gave up trying to improve his own game. Until he died in 2002, he was a popular speaker at conventions of PGA teaching professionals, and sometimes we appeared on the same program. One day in Toronto, I listened as Paul spoke to a gathering of Canadian professionals, a gathering he had spoken to the previous year. He was, by then, around ninety years old.

"Thank you so much for bringing me back. I'm thrilled to be here again this year," Paul began. "But I have to apologize to you. Last year I promised you that I was going to practice my short game for at least two hours every day. I promised you I was going to honor that commitment."

I wondered where he was going with this. I knew Paul liked to challenge his fellow teaching pros to work to improve their own games and promise that he would do the same. He believed that working to improve their own games made pros better teachers. But I wasn't sure why he was apologizing.

"I'm embarrassed to tell you that on three days last year, I did not honor my commitment. I hope you all did better than I did," Paul said.

The room was silent, the club pros thinking about a nonagenarian practicing his short game 362 days in the past year. I had two thoughts. One, I was blown away by Paul's dedication to honoring his commitment. And two, how was I going to follow that in my own talk?

I tell the story to illustrate how seriously exceptional people take the commitments they make to themselves. Paul Runyan is only one example.

I talked a while back with Pete Sampras, who won fourteen major singles titles during his illustrious tennis career. Pete turned pro at sixteen and won the U.S. Open at nineteen, in 1990. He was a good player at a young age. But he didn't win another major title for two years following that U.S. Open. In his own mind, the turning point in his career came when he lost in the 1992 U.S. Open final to Stefan Edberg.

He went home and stayed in bed for three days, brooding over the feeling that he hadn't been giving tennis his best effort. He wondered if he wanted to make the commitment necessary to see if he could be great. Was he willing to put in the time and the effort and be single-minded in that quest? He decided that he was.

And for the next eight years or so, Pete honored that commitment. He was in his early twenties, making lots of money, traveling to glamorous places like Paris and London to play. But as he recalled it, he lived almost monastically in that period. His life revolved around training and competing. During tennis's brief off-season, he didn't take a break. He moved into a condo in Florida where he and his coach, Paul Annacone, could practice for hours each day in high heat and humidity.

After that time at the top, Pete's commitment waned. He wanted a more rounded life. He married in 2000 and he and his wife, actress Bridgette Wilson, started a family. His tennis results started to slip. He rallied himself for one last summer of commitment with Annacone in 2002, and he scored an upset victory in the U.S. Open that September. But he realized that he no longer wanted to devote the time and energy required to be the best tennis player he could be. Wisely, he retired at the top. Without honoring his commitment, he knew he would be just another player, and he didn't want that.

When I work with exceptional people, I always see this sort of devotion to commitment. I see it with my friend Gary Burkhead, who retired from the financial services industry and committed himself to becoming a scratch golfer, even though his handicap when he retired was nowhere near single digits. Most people don't think of their golden years as a time to make a serious commitment to a self-improvement program, but Gary does. Because of his commitment, he takes lessons. He practices. He plays. He lifts weights and stretches. He practices some more. He is moving inexorably toward his goal. When a problem arises, Gary is a problem solver. He finds a new teacher, a new gym routine, a new practice regimen—whatever it takes to keep making progress. When I last checked in with him, he was working through back and knee problems. Knowing Gary, I know he will spend all night on the Internet if he has to in order to find the trainer or doctor who can help him overcome these issues and keep practicing and playing. The notion that he's over seventy and ought to take it easy doesn't occur to him. He's not going to give in to the idea that he's old. That's not how he does things. I find it fascinating to watch him, and I find it easy to understand how he was successful in the financial world. Whether you're trying to run a successful business or lower your golf score, the method is the same. Devise an improvement plan and commit yourself to it. Persevere.

Gary has been shooting in the low seventies the last few times I've checked in with him; he's had one competitive 69. I told him, only partly in jest, that the next problem he'll have to deal with is going to be people telling him how lucky he is to be so naturally gifted at golf. That's because people will look at someone achieving what Gary is achieving, and they won't want to believe it's because of something they could do themselves, like keeping a commitment. So they choose to think it's because God endowed Gary with some special gift. They're fooling themselves.

Sometimes, the commitment of exceptional people can seem extreme. I work with Chad Knaus, the crew chief for Jimmie Johnson's NASCAR team at Hendrick Motorsports, winners of six NASCAR Sprint Cup titles. Chad consistently works ninety- to one-hundred-hour weeks, poring over every detail of the race car's preparation, from the pistons to the paint job. This kind of commitment comes at a price. Although Chad says he wants to be a married man and a father, he hasn't as yet found a way to make a relationship run as well or as long as the number forty-eight car he prepares for Jimmie. He's on a mission to become the greatest crew chief in NASCAR history, and until he's done that, it looks as if marriage and family will have to wait. He tells me he might wind up at fifty-five or sixty, married to a twenty-five-year-old. And he might. A person who is capable of keeping a commitment the way Chad does is capable of almost anything.

I took Keegan Bradley (Pat's nephew and the 2011 PGA champion) to meet John Calipari and the University of Kentucky basketball team a couple of years ago. We had dinner with Cal, and Keegan asked if he could see Cal's office, which is high above Rupp Arena, with a picture window that affords a view of the floor. We got there at eleven thirty at night. Cal opened the curtains and we saw Anthony Davis and Michael Kidd-Gilchrist down on the court, practicing. Keegan is himself a very committed athlete, but even he was impressed by the dedication and commitment that had Anthony and Michael out on the court practicing as midnight approached.

How do athletes like Anthony, Michael, and Keegan keep their commitments while their peers slack off? It's a combination of things.

The easiest way to keep a commitment is to love what you're doing, as Anthony and Michael love basketball and Keegan loves golf. But you have to love the entirety of what you're doing, not just the occasional glory and rewards. I remember a few years ago, Tom Kite and I were asked to speak about attitude to a group of PGA Tour rookies. Tom spoke first. "I'm going to let Doc do most of the talking," he said. "I'm only going to tell y'all one thing."

I was immediately eager to know what the one thing was. Tom didn't disappoint me.

"If you're going to play the Tour, you have to love golf *all the time*," he said. "It's not going to work if you can only love it when everything's going your way, every putt's going in the hole, and every carom is bouncing into the fairway instead of out of bounds. It's not going to work if you practice every day and only love it when the ball is going where you're looking. You've got to love it when you practice day after day after day and you can't find it. You've got to love it when every putt looks like it's going in and then lips out. That's what it's about."

There wasn't much I had to say after that. If the youngsters got nothing else from that session, they'd learned something extremely important.

You might say, "Well, of course, it's easy to love golf."

But it really isn't, at least if it's competitive golf. I run into people all the time who tell me how much they love golf. Some of them are clients. They'll sit down in my basement and say, "I'm so glad I'm here, because I love golf."

These clients love reading about golf. They love watching tournaments on television. They love taking lessons and practicing. But after I talk with them awhile, a crack opens in this facade. They tell me they're realizing something, and that is that they love golf all the time except when they're actually playing in a tournament. When they get into a tournament, they feel like they're locked in a Siberian prison camp waiting to be shot.

This is a problem. It's a problem akin to having a spouse who loves you—except when you're together.

It's a problem because golf, like every competitive endeavor, is going to test and try the person who wishes to be exceptional. There are going to be times when, as Tom said, all the putts lip out, all the bounces go out of bounds, and the harder you practice the worse it gets. Golf is not unique in this respect. The best financial consultant is going to have weeks when none of his sales calls work out and none of the investments he recommends go up. The best doctors are going to have periods when none of the patients get better. If they're going to sustain their commitments during such times, it helps if they truly love what they're doing, even when nothing is going right. They're engrossed in it. It fascinates them. It never feels like work.

I understand that not everyone is lucky enough to feel that way all the time. But what I see in exceptional people is the will to learn to love what they're committed to doing. Skeptics might dismiss learning to love something as delusional. Skeptics, though, don't understand either the power or the malleability of the subconscious. You can learn to love something if you make an effort to focus on the aspects of that activity that please you, thinking over and over again about how much you enjoy them.

Let's take, for example, a theoretical lumberjack. He got

into logging because he loved the forest and loved being out-doors. He loved the feeling that by selecting the right trees for cutting, he was being a good steward and helping the forest stay healthy. But as the years went by, this fictional lumber-jack stopped noticing the smells and sights of the forest, the birds and the animals, and the clean air. He got bored with cutting trees. He decided he hated the sound of a power saw. Pretty soon he started telling himself he hated being a lumber-jack. His productivity fell. He was in danger of losing his job.

If he came to me at this point, I would tell him he had two choices. He could quit being a lumberjack and find some other line of work. Or he could fall in love with it again. He could start deliberately noticing the forest again. He could find ways to renew his pride in his work. And, maybe, he could get a set of earplugs to mute the sound of the saw.

The reality is that while a few of us are lucky enough to do something we can nearly always love, like playing golf, most of us find that there are things we like and things we don't like about our careers. I've known public school teachers who loved working with kids, loved helping them get a better start in life than they might otherwise have. Because of that love, they were committed to improving as teachers, to communi-cating with parents, to working long hours, to learning new, better classroom management techniques and devising more effective lesson plans. When I taught at the University of Vir-ginia, I always loved working with students and with athletes and helping them improve. I enjoyed the research and the teaching. I could have done without the paperwork I was re-quired to submit by the university administration. In the same way, committed and dedicated public school teachers can loathe the staff meetings and paperwork they are too often burdened with. The only recourse in this situation is to focus relentlessly on the aspects of the job you love. If you can't, it's often best to consider changing jobs.

I understand, of course, that people can't always be committed to something they love, much as I wish they could. There are always going to be times when you have to commit yourself to doing something that doesn't appeal to you. This is one of the biggest lessons school is supposed to teach us. There are subjects we like and do well at with relative ease. There are subjects we struggle with. For me, that subject was math. I remember frequently being astounded when a teacher wrote a new kind of equation with a blank in it on the blackboard and one of my classmates instantly raised her hand and gave the answer. My head was still swimming. I never learned to love math, but I learned that if I committed myself to working at it, after a few weeks, the answers would start coming to me as well. My dad's strict policy requiring As and Bs in order to play sports helped here, too. It's always good to have support if you need to keep a commitment.

It's important to note that a commitment to working on self-improvement doesn't have to be quite as demanding as Paul Runyan's commitment to working on his short game. That level of commitment and dedication worked well for Paul, but it wouldn't work well for everybody. If a golfer on the PGA Tour told me he needed to take a week off every six weeks or so to leave the clubs in the garage and enjoy his family, I would have no objection. Excelling at any athletic endeavor demands a commitment to work persistently at the fundamentals and to long hours of practice in between competitions. There's an old saying that you sweat in practice so you don't bleed in the game, and it carries a lot of truth. But there is room for the occasional break. It's in fact necessary to build breaks into strenuous routines to allow the body to recharge and to avoid injury from overwork.

But in general, I find most people have a lot more trouble with perseverance than they do with taking breaks. It's easy to decide to change direction in your life. But any important change requires hard work over time. It could be a short time. That's happened. But it is more likely to take a longer time. It's more likely that there will be setbacks and plateaus along the way. The higher one's aspirations, the more likely this is to be true. If someone who can't break 100 on the golf course comes to me and says he'd like to be able to shoot 85, the journey is likely to be relatively brief. That's because the 100 shooter probably has a few fundamental flaws in his swing and doesn't practice his short game. If I can get him to take a few lessons from a good pro to improve his swing and to spend some quality time at the practice green chipping and pitching, I can be fairly confident he'll reach his goal in a year or two. But if the 100 shooter wants to be a scratch player, the task requires a lot more perseverance. It's simply harder to go from 85 to scratch than it is to go from 100 to 85, even though the numbers tell you the two journeys cover the same distance. That's true in most areas. If you know nothing about the piano, you can learn to play a few songs competently a lot faster than you can go from playing a few songs competently to being a concert-level performer. That takes tremendous perseverance.

How do exceptional people find this perseverance?

First of all, they make up their minds that they value being persistent. I remember learning of this attitude in the 1960s, when I read an excellent book about Bill Bradley, then a basketball player at Princeton. The book was called *A Sense of Where You Are*, by John McPhee, and it helped cement Bradley's place among the role models I chose as a kid. He excelled both athletically and academically, as I wanted to do. He said something in that book about persistent effort that stuck with me: "If I'm better than you now and I practice more than you every day, how could you ever hope to catch me?"

Athletes and champions decide to take pride in their persistence and patience. They understand that in any endeavor, there will be setbacks. They know better than to take these setbacks personally, to let them diminish their belief in themselves.

Most of them have learned to take a big goal and break it into small steps. Suppose you're now a couch potato, but you set yourself a goal to compete in and complete a full Ironman triathlon—swimming 2.4 miles in open water, running a 26.2-mile marathon, and biking 112 miles, one right after another. It's a formidable challenge. If you started out by trying to do a full triathlon, you'd probably give up midway through the bike or marathon segment, assuming you didn't drown during the open-water swim. But, of course, you wouldn't do that. You'd start out training in a pool, extending your distance by a lap or so every week. You'd begin with ten-mile bike rides, working gradually to a century. And so on. Doing it this way has several advantages when it comes to perseverance. It gives you a process to follow. It gives you a series of intermediate goals. And it gives you the satisfaction of meeting these smaller challenges along the way. If your goal is to get a little stronger and a little fitter every day, it's easier to see the sort of progress that helps sustain a commitment.

This is, if you think about it, the way we learn most things we take up in childhood. A toddler learns to read one-syllable words, then to read books with pictures, then "chapter books" and young adult fiction before moving on to the great books and, perhaps, a dissertation on literature. Advancing to the dissertation stage doesn't seem like such an enormous leap, because it's done gradually. Perseverance comes a little easier.

But a lot of people fail to fully understand the nature of this step-by-step process. They want to jump to the end. When my daughter, Casey, was in the fourth grade, her teacher invited me to come and talk to the kids about writing books. I started out by asking them to remember when they first learned to write the letter A. They learned the capital A and the small a. Then they learned to put letters together and make words like "dog" and "cat." Then they learned to put a few words together in a simple sentence. A year or so later, they learned to combine sentences into paragraphs. Then, as they reached the age of ten or so, they started learning to combine paragraphs into short essays. The book-writing process, I said, was like writing essays every day for a year. With patience and persistence, the work becomes a book.

A little boy raised his hand.

"Yeah," he said. "But how do you find a publisher?"

The tendency to want to jump to the end is ingrained early. We have to use our will to apply ourselves, instead, to the process.

I have always believed in free will. I'm not sure where in the brain and body the characteristic called free will can be located, and maybe it doesn't spring from a particular lobe in an individual brain but from a matrix of places within the brain. But I believe God endowed us with free will and that we can use it to stay the course toward any goal we set for ourselves. However, using free will doesn't necessarily mean that we grit our teeth every day and force ourselves to do something we find unpleasant. That kind of willpower consumes a lot of energy, and it's extremely difficult to summon it on a daily basis for a period of months or years.

Another way to think of perseverance is to consider it a set of good habits directed at whatever goal you want to accomplish. Habits are powerful forces in our lives. When we act from habit, we don't need the grit-your-teeth type of willpower. We just do something without thinking much about it. It's almost a reflex. Exceptional people tend to have habits that help them achieve what they want. People who are struggling tend to have habits that undermine them. It may be more useful to see free will not as a means of gritting your teeth and forcing yourself to do something, but as a tool you can use to make an intelligent, informed effort to change your habits.

Let's suppose that you're a person who wants to be fitter. You have a time-consuming job and a family that needs your attention. The only time you have each day for a workout is between eight thirty and ten in the evening. There's no shortage of workout opportunities available to you at that hour. You pay dues to a health club a few blocks away from your home. It's got a gym and a pool. Your neighborhood has a park with a good jogging trail. You could get out every evening for a workout that would, over time, allow you to achieve your goal.

But habits get in your way. When you get home from work, you like to have a cocktail; it helps you unwind. Then there's a glass of wine at dinner. You like ice cream for dessert, and you generally have some. So by the time you finish your meal you feel heavy, full, and a little inebriated. You leave the table and pass by the easy chair in front of the big-screen TV you bought a few years ago. You habitually decide to check out what's on, thinking you might spend a few minutes watching a program. You see a commercial for popcorn or pizza, and you get a little craving. Pretty soon, you're snacking in front of the television. Time goes by and the opportunity for a workout has gone. You've got to go to sleep if you're going to be able to rise in time for work.

And so it goes. Habit has defeated your intention to be fitter and your commitment to a daily workout. Indeed, it's made you a little less fit, due to the alcohol, the ice cream, and the snack.

Thanks to research over the past few decades, we now know more about habits and what it takes to change them. We know that habit is rooted in the subconscious mind. As I've indicated, understanding the ways to use the subconscious mind is extremely important in exceptionality. One of the keys to success for athletes, musicians, surgeons, and anyone whose work involves fine motor skills is learning to allow the subconscious mind to govern the application of those skills. A good golfer plays his best when he doesn't consciously think about the mechanics of the swing when he is hitting the ball. A concert violinist produces his best music when he stops thinking about where his fingers go and just lets the music flow out of him. I've seen heart surgeons listen to music and chat about their golf games when they've got a patient on the table with his beating heart exposed. It's not that they don't care about the patient's fate. It just that they've learned that with a scalpel in their hands and a life on the line, it's best to let their subconscious govern the movements they've trained for many years to perform.

Training, of course, is essential. If you've never been to medical school, you're not going to perform successful heart surgery just by grabbing a scalpel and letting your subconscious take over. Your subconscious will guide your body through a good golf swing only if you've taken lessons and practiced—a lot. The principle I teach to golfers and other athletes is "Train it and trust it," which means "Learn the skill thoroughly, so it's ingrained in your subconscious. Then, at the moment of performance, don't think about it. Trust that your subconscious brain will do its job." But the trusting won't work if the training hasn't happened. Nor will it work if you confuse the subconscious with negative thoughts, fears, or doubts. No matter how much practice a golfer has done to groove a good putting stroke and routine, his stroke will change for the worse if he's doubtful or fearful about a putt. He has to be confident, to believe in his abilities.

Even if you're not a surgeon or a professional athlete, you've got motor skills that you've trained your subconscious mind to execute. If, for example, you drive a car with a manual transmission, you were probably quite clumsy about shifting gears when you started. Your car bucked and probably stalled for a while as you learned. But after a while, you mastered it, and the motor skill was ingrained in your subconscious mind. Now you shift gears smoothly without consciously thinking about it. You may complete a drive to work and not even remember shifting gears, though you did so many times. Your conscious mind, meanwhile, is free to have a conversation with a passenger or listen to the radio.

A habit is, in effect, a circuit rooted in the subconscious mind. It consists of a cue, a behavior governed by the subconscious in response to that cue, and a reward that reinforces the behavior. The cue can be anything that triggers a habitual behavior. A cue can be blatant, like an ad for pizza or potato chips that you see on TV. A cue can be subtle. Maybe it's just the feeling of fatigue and stress you experience when you come home from work, coupled with the sight of the cabinet where you keep your liquor. It can be the residual taste of salt and fat on your tongue after you've consumed a potato chip, a cue that prompts you to eat more. There's a reason why potato chip manufacturers advertise, "Bet you can't eat just one." They know that the first chip leaves a taste on your tongue that stimulates a habitual response—eating another one.

Maybe the cue is a feeling of ennui as the evening progresses. Your subconscious responds to that cue by directing your body to execute a habitual response—turning on the television. You don't consciously consider the best option for your evening. You find yourself sitting in front of the television without having given it much, if any, thought. It's not a considered decision made by your conscious mind. It's a habit governed by the subconscious. Your reward is a vague, soporific feeling that displaces the restless ennui that was your cue.

Unhelpful behaviors become ingrained precisely because they produce a reward. This is very similar to the training effect in the golf swing. As we practice and train, we get feedback from the way the golf ball performs after we swing at it. The desired ball flight reinforces the subconscious feel of the correct swing. It becomes ingrained, and the golfer can produce it without consciously thinking about how to do it.

But this dynamic between mind and body also explains why bad habits are so hard to break. When we're snacking, to take a common example, we ingest fats, salts, and sugars, all of which produce quick, temporary, but pleasant chemical changes in your body. Alcohol can soothe nerves or, at least temporarily, satisfy a craving for alcohol. The subconscious registers these pleasures without critically evaluating them, and the bad habit is continually reinforced, just as the good golf swing is reinforced through proper practice.

Unfortunately, the research suggests that you can never completely eliminate a bad habit once it's ingrained in the subconscious. That's why it's always possible to relapse into bad habits—procrastinating instead of working, watching television instead of working out, and so on. But while you may not be able to erase the subconscious circuit that constitutes a bad habit, you can overlay it with a good habit, using your free will and an intelligent analysis of your habits. This process is almost the exact opposite of the way an informed athlete wants to use his mind during competition. The athlete wants the subconscious to take over from the conscious mind during performance. The person trying to establish a new, constructive habit wants the conscious mind to overrule the subconscious.

The first step is identifying the cues that trigger habitual, bad behaviors. To continue with the example of the man who wants to be fitter, let's suppose part of his plan is to stop riding a cart and walk the golf course every time he plays. Sounds good. But he and his regular foursome generally stop at the clubhouse bar after a round of golf to have a beer. There's nothing wrong with this. But let's suppose the bad habit that stems from this is that he typically has three or four beers instead of one and consumes an unhealthy amount of the peanuts and pretzels the bartender puts on each foursome's table. Golf, which he intended as a healthy activity, is turned into an unhealthy one by this bad habit.

There probably are a number of cues involved in this bad habit. In the first place, he's probably hungry and thirsty after he comes off the course, especially if he's walked. Hunger and thirst are cues that prompt him to drink and eat. Maybe his friends' beers are a cue for him to have one, just to be sociable. More than likely, there's yet another cue, the pleasant little buzz he gets from the first beer, a buzz that prompts his subconscious brain to want more. And finally, there's the residual taste of the salt from the bar snacks. It also prompts his sub-conscious to want to drink and eat more. Eating and drinking more produces a temporary sensation of pleasure, which is the reward that reinforces the bad habit. So does the loosening of social inhibitions that seems to make the conversation wittier.

Once our man has identified these cues and his subcon-scious responses, he must either eliminate the cues or plan different responses to them. Eliminating the cues is rarely possible. If your cue is the sight of the television at the end of a long day, you're probably not going to be able to throw the TV in the trash, particularly if you want to maintain good relations with the rest of your household. If your cue is an ad for pizza, you could theoretically move to a country where pizza isn't a staple and the language barrier keeps you from watching and reading media that carry pizza ads. But that would be an extreme and probably impractical solution. Most of your cues are not going away.

The more likely path to success is to fashion a new response to the cues that trigger bad habits. Let's return to our golfer who'd like to break the habit of having three or four beers and an unhealthy quantity of peanuts and pretzels at the end of his rounds. When he realizes that the immediate cues are hunger and thirst, he can mobilize his conscious brain to do several things. For starters, he can try to take care of the hunger and thirst in healthy ways. He can drink more water on the course and order a big glass of soda water when he enters the bar. He can mobilize his conscious mind and determine that he'll con-sume the water before he drinks the first sip of beer. Similarly, with the hunger, he can decide to have a high-protein breakfast before he goes to the course and then order something healthy when he comes into the bar. Maybe a salad.

What you're doing, as you begin to build a better habit, is enlisting your conscious mind to overrule the subconscious impulse that is the crux of your bad habit. Thinking through the cues that trigger your unwanted behaviors is one way to engage the conscious mind and remind it to become engaged again when the cues actually happen.

Exceptional people seem to seek out cues that in most people would trigger a bad habit and use them as a tool to reinforce good habits. Some people would look out the window and see rain and think, "Well, I guess I don't have to practice golf today. I can play a video game." An exceptional person would see the same rain and go out to practice, relishing the opportunity to improve his ability to cope with wet grips and squishy ground underfoot. He'd see it as a chance to get a practice advantage over rivals who would take the day off. Someone who wants to be exceptional at basketball sees a snowfall as an opportunity to shovel off the court, practice, and get better on a day when her peers and potential rivals will be inside, not getting better. An exceptional person who's into fitness and a healthy diet will relish the chance to go to a banquet, which is the sort of occasion that cues a lot of people to drink and eat too much. The exceptional person sees it as a chance to demonstrate, if only to himself, the power of his will. He takes pride in doing things average people will not do. And pride is one of the rewards that reinforces a good habit.

There are three other things our theoretical habit changer can do to reinforce the emerging, new, good habit.

He can enlist the support of people around him. Take the example of the golfer who wants to limit what he eats and drinks after his round. If the bartender is a regular, he can tell the bartender he wants to limit himself to one beer. He can ask the bartender not to put the peanuts and pretzels on the table within easy reach. Maybe he can ask the others in his foursome if they mind forgoing the snack food entirely. He can tell them he's got to limit himself to one beer. They'd probably just tease him if he broke down and ordered a second, but the prospect of teasing is a good deterrent against the reemergence of the bad habit.

In general, it's helpful to enlist support when you're trying to create a new good habit. A spouse or sibling or roommate can be helpful. People hire personal trainers because they know the trainer can be helpful. And, of course, mutual support is a big part of team sports. You can think of the coaches and the teammates as a support group helping to instill good habits, because that's what they are—at least on good teams.

Visualization can also help. I've talked about visualization as a way for athletes to get comfortable with succeeding in a new situation, by contemplating, at length and with vivid detail, the way it would feel to win the Masters, to take one example. But it's possible to use visualization to help our performance in virtually any situation. In the case of the golfer and the post-round beers, our golfer could visualize himself going through the usual routine—coming off the golf course hungry and thirsty, ordering a salad and a club soda, staying away from the peanuts and pretzels, limiting himself to one beer, and so on. This kind of visualization seems to act almost like an alarm bell. When the golfer encounters the circumstances he's visualized, the alarm goes off, reminding the conscious brain, rather than the subconscious brain, to engage and determine the way the golfer responds to the cues.

I've known this technique to be helpful in breaking a cigarette habit. Smokers often "quit" many times, but after they've stopped for a couple of weeks or even a month, their best efforts are sabotaged by an unplanned, impulsive cigarette that is a response to a powerful cue they're not ready for. They light up without thinking about it as their subconscious responds to a cue. The cue might be academic anxiety on the night before a big final exam. It might be a moment of social anxiety at a party where others are smoking and the person who's trying to quit has had a couple of drinks. (The drinks make it harder to engage the conscious brain to govern behavior.) Before the smoker knows it, he's had several cigarettes and the effort and abstinence of a month are wasted.

The smoker in this example needs to analyze the moments when he's most susceptible to having an unplanned, impulsive cigarette. Then he can visualize those moments and plan a response that doesn't include lighting up. As always with visualization, the more effort that goes into it, the greater the effect that comes out of it. A hurried thought on the way to a party is not nearly as likely to be effective as taking five minutes in a quiet, dark room to imagine the upcoming party with all of its sounds, sights, and smells. Imagine as vividly as possible the vaguely gnawing feeling of meeting new people, feeling nervous, and smelling cigarette smoke. Then imagine the substitute behavior. Maybe it's stepping outside onto a patio and breathing clean, fresh air. Maybe it's having a soda. Maybe it's just the feeling of satisfaction attained by recognizing a moment of temptation and resisting it. Whatever it is, it needs to be rewarding in some way. Visualization will help ensure that when the moment of crisis comes, the new behavior will be remembered and executed.

It may also help reinforce a new, good habit if you chart or otherwise make a written record of the new behavior. Let's take one of the most pernicious bad habits, procrastination. I talk to many people, particularly in the business world, who tell me their performance suffers because instead of getting right to their work and working steadily throughout the day, they procrastinate. They answer e-mails, surf the Web, chat with colleagues, or otherwise find ways to put off writing that report, making those calls, or whatever the day's work is. Then, at the end of the day, they find themselves unable to complete their work. Or they finish it hastily and sloppily, undermining its effectiveness.

The cue for this procrastination might be the feeling of anxiety or insecurity that often accompanies the prospect of doing challenging work. Maybe, if your work entails making sales calls, it's the fear of rejection. Your subconscious has learned that reading the newspaper or surfing the Web is a way of putting this unpleasant feeling in abeyance for an hour or two. Your subconscious is not so good at reasoning that the short-term gain from procrastination is not worth the long-term pain from failing to do your work on time and well.

The old-fashioned to-do list is one way to graphically reinforce the conscious behavior you want to replace procrastination. It's a way of imposing your conscious will in place of the subconscious habit circuit that prevents you from getting your work done. It might be even more effective if you put a time next to each item on your daily list, indicating the deadline for its completion. Again, breaking the task list down into small components is often helpful. If, for instance, your goal is to write a thousand-word paper by one p.m., it might be easier if you plan to have the first two hundred words written by nine a.m., the second two hundred by ten a.m., etc. In place of a list, you might have a graph, indicating how many calls you make between the start of business and lunch. Checking items off your to-do list or entering the numbers that show your work is itself an immediate reward for the behavior you're trying to reinforce. It's a way to let your conscious brain determine your behavior and, gradually, through many repetitions, make that behavior a habit. Writing down good behaviors helps impart the sense of pride and satisfaction that exceptional people use as the fundamental reward for the habits that make them successful.

It's tremendously important to keep your goals in mind as much as you can. Most New Year's resolutions fall by the wayside when people lose sight of their goals. The conscious brain is engaged when we think about goals. The subconscious takes over when we stop thinking about them. If your goal, for instance, is to stop eating sugared foods, you can't let yourself get so engrossed in other daily activities that you lose sight of your goal and wind up with a cookie in your mouth before you know it.

This isn't easy to do. In a busy person's life, there are lots of competing demands for conscious attention. In my own life, I get engrossed in the people I'm working with. I devote all my attention to their issues. And I'm not always successful at keeping my goals for diet and exercise in mind. But I am very good at catching myself if I get half an inch away from the path I am trying to stay on.

You're not perfect. Your commitment and perseverance will not be perfect. You're going to have setbacks and stumbles in pursuing any goal you set. The important thing is not that you have these setbacks but how you react to them. Perseverance doesn't mean perfection. It's not often constant, unwavering adherence to a commitment. Instead, it is usually a series of quick course corrections when you get off track.

I'm reminded of John Calipari when I met him. He was coaching the basketball team at the University of Massachusetts. His motto then was "Refuse to Lose." That puzzled some people. None of Cal's UMass teams went undefeated. How could he say they refused to lose?

Refusing to lose, though, doesn't mean you're never going to come out on the short end of a particular game. It doesn't mean your commitments will never be broken. It doesn't mean your perseverance won't occasionally waver. It doesn't mean that bad habits won't occasionally reemerge.

It means that you never give up. You never give in to doubt, fear, or fatigue. Giving up is the only true loss.

6.

Dreams, Goals, and Process

THE DREAM has become a staple of broadcast journalism. Let someone win something, whether it's an Emmy, or a Little League championship, or America's Next Top Model, and the announcer is all but certain to proclaim that that person's dream has come true. Every kid on *American Idol* is chasing a dream, even if he can't quite chase down the melody.

I am the last person to denigrate the importance of dreams. I know how powerful they can be as motivators. I know how devastating their absence can be. I had a client recently tell me that his golf career has stalled. "I think I messed up a bit, Doc," he said. "All I ever wanted to do was play on the PGA Tour. I dreamed about it. So I wanted to be my club champ, and I won that. And I wanted to win my state amateur, and I won that. I wanted to get a college scholarship, and I did. I wanted to be an All-American, and I was. Those were all steps to the PGA Tour. And then I got to the Tour, and

I was just happy to be there. And now I feel like I'm just going through the motions."

Without a dream, it's hard to be motivated. But it's also true that dreams are cheap. Lots of people who never achieve much have dreams. Exceptional people also have dreams. But exceptional people go well beyond dreaming.

The essential difference was implied by the chronology my stalled golfer gave me. He didn't just dream about being on the PGA Tour. His dream helped him see a ladder, a ladder that started with his club championship and led to the PGA Tour. It had intermediate rungs. In order to climb each rung, he committed himself to a process.

That ability to take a dream and use it to create a process is what separates exceptional people from mere dreamers.

John Calipari helped me understand this. When he was just starting in college coaching, Cal wrote down some big dreams. He wanted to be a head coach by the age of thirty. He wanted to win a national championship by the age of thirty-five. And so on. Cal has never lacked for ambition and belief in himself.

He put the card on which he wrote those dreams away. A few years ago, his son found it. When he saw what his younger self had written, Cal was a little uncomfortable. The dreams he had written down seemed to his more mature self a little self-absorbed and superficial. Instead, over the years, Cal has come to believe in and aspire to what I call process goals, which serve dreams. He calls this "the grind." He strives to work hard and get better every day. He tries to persuade his players to do the same, to build their bodies and build their skills every day. He strives to teach them the importance of defense, rebounding, hustle, and team play. He tries to teach them to love and embrace that grind. He knows that if his teams do embrace the grind—the process—they'll find out if they can win championships. And indeed they have. Sometimes they win Southeastern Conference championships. Sometimes they win national championships. But Cal, in contrast to his younger self, now realizes that it's the process that's most important, not the results. Sometimes teams that adhere to a great process lose, as Cal's Kentucky team did when it came up against UConn in the finals of the most recent NCAA tournament. Regardless of how Kentucky does in the postseason, though, Cal is satisfied if he feels that he and his team have done their best to get better every day along the way. He can't ultimately control who wins the conference and who wins the NCAA tournament. There are going to be years when other teams are simply better. But he can control the grind and the way every person in the Kentucky program devotes himself to that grind. And he does.

I don't want to get hung up on semantics here. The word "grind" might put some people off. If you want to call it "the ladder," and that feels more congenial to you, go right ahead. "Goals" can put other people off. Tom Kite used to tell me that he preferred to think of dreams, because he felt that dreams were his and his alone. Goals, he thought, were things that other people imposed on him. The important fact was not what Tom called them but how he acted. He embraced and loved the grind, the process of becoming the best player he could be.

Let's go back to the example of the would-be triathlete. Winning an Olympic triathlon medal might be called either a dream or a goal. The terminology is not important. What's important is whether the dream or goal gives birth to a process. You can imagine what that process might be. It would involve lots of training—every day. It would involve finding coaches to refine technique and devise workouts in swimming, biking, and running. It would involve enlisting a nutrition expert to help make sure that the athlete had precisely the fuel he needed. It would involve working with doctors, trainers, and massage therapists so that the body could withstand the rigor of the program and grow fitter. It might involve a sports psychologist. It might involve joining a club or in some way working to build a supportive group of people. Most importantly, it would involve setting daily and even hourly goals—swim so many yards before breakfast, run so many miles before lunch, bike a certain number of miles in the afternoon, go to the gym and complete a stretching and lifting workout before dinner. These daily challenges are process goals.

Exceptional people immerse themselves in process goals. They care most about how well they follow their chosen process every day. They don't have to be chasing Olympic medals. When I was a young coach and teacher, I didn't dream about how many major golf championship winners I would eventually coach. I just wanted to help people as best I could day by day. I always felt that if I took care of coaching people and helping them become as good as they could be, my life would take care of itself and I'd have a ball. That turned out to be true, and to be one of the smarter decisions I ever made.

Without making and sustaining a commitment to an effective process, an individual cannot know her potential. Sometimes golfers will come to me, talk for a while, and play a round of golf with me. Then they'll ask me whether I think their dreams are attainable. I almost always say that we'll only know the answer to that question after they've committed themselves to a process that will improve their games and sustained that commitment for a long time. My advice, after recommending that process, is that they put no limits on themselves or what they think they can accomplish.

It's important to remember that the goals you set for yourself are, in some ways, also limits. If, for example, you decide that your goal at work is to make $150,000 in commissions during the coming year, the likelihood is that you will approach $150,000, assuming you also have a commitment to a good daily work process. But I rarely see anyone who exceeds the goal he's set for himself.

It's all right at the beginning of a process to set goals that are lower than your ultimate aspiration. For instance, if you're a poor bunker player, and you commit yourself to improving that aspect of your golf game, I don't mind if your first goal is merely to get ten balls in a row out of the practice bunker and onto the green. Your next goal should be to get a lot of them close to the flagstick. Ultimately, your goal might be to hole a certain percentage or to get more than half of your bunker shots up and down. An aspiring touring pro would want ultimately to set his goals higher still. But there's nothing wrong with the step-by-step approach, as long as it points steadily upward.

There is something wrong with setting low ultimate goals. Sometimes players facing a tournament on a course with fast, tricky greens tell me one of their goals for the week is not to three-putt. And their practice process for that tournament involves a lot of lag putting, where they're just trying to get the first putt to stop close to the hole.

If you hate three-putting and you make your ultimate goal avoiding three-putts, you'll two-putt your life away. I wear the ears off the players I counsel telling them that they had better love one-putting more than they hate three-putting. I want them to envision every putt they try going in the hole, no matter how long or slippery the putt is. I want them to try to make everything. I tell them that every great player I have ever known has three-putted. Great players understand that. They don't care how they look or what people say when they three-putt. They also know that the weeks when they sink a lot of long putts and make nearly all their four-footers are the weeks when they win money and championships. They set their goals to help them have more of those weeks.

I saw the same principle at work when I taught at the University of Virginia. Some kids got to UVA and thought they had reached their goal. They just wanted to survive and graduate, and for the most part, that's what they did. Other kids got to UVA and saw it as a stepping stone to Harvard Medical School. Those kids took the hardest courses they could find. They wanted an A+ in all of them, and they worked very hard for those grades. I had students with high goals who would write papers over and over until they earned the grade they wanted. It didn't matter to them if their peers were spending the weekend going to concerts and football games. Their goals compelled them. Their goals helped them determine and follow a process that led to excellent grades. Their goals helped them learn to manage their time. A lot of these highly motivated kids were athletes as well as students; they made time for both pursuits. They went to Virginia because it was a place that would enable them to pursue a world-class education at the same time they participated in collegiate athletics at the highest level. And when they got into Harvard Medical School, it was no accident.

I think one of the most interesting aspects of Tiger Woods's career has been the impact he's evidently had on the goals of his rivals. When Tiger came on the scene, he acknowledged publicly that he'd grown up with Jack Nicklaus's picture on the wall of his bedroom, and his dream was to break Jack's record of eighteen major championships. I admire Tiger tremendously for having the guts to say it. But when I hear the generation of players who are coming just behind Tiger talk about their goals, I don't hear any of them talk about Jack's record. I hear the next generation of top players say they'd like to get to number one in the world rankings. But they don't talk about nineteen majors. Maybe it's because Tiger is still chasing that number. Maybe it's because the difficulties Tiger has had getting past fourteen have a daunting effect on the psyches of other players.

Now, there's nothing wrong with setting the top ranking as your goal. It's a tremendous challenge, and I appreciate the work that players put in just to get there for a while. I understand that just because a player doesn't talk publicly about a goal like nineteen majors doesn't mean he hasn't set it for himself privately. Still, I wish a lot more players would stop being "realistic" when they dream. I believe that if Jack had won twenty-five majors and Tiger had set out to surpass him, Tiger would have twenty by now. That's the nature of goals and dreams.

In sports or in business, if you're not aspiring to dominate, to be the very best, you're coasting. And you can only coast in one direction.

Yet, most people, in my experience, choose to be average. I met a man at the University of Connecticut when I was a young coach and grad student, working with the lacrosse program. He coached another sport. My first year at UConn, we went to the NCAA tournament, which at the time had a field of about eight teams. It was the best year UConn had ever had in lacrosse. About a week after our season ended, this coach invited me to lunch. I happily accepted, because I love talking to experienced coaches about their wisdom. I am always trying to learn.

But what this coach had to say startled and disappointed me. He started off telling me what a great job we were doing with the lacrosse program. He noted that we had begun fall and winter training sessions and we'd started doing a much more aggressive effort in recruiting. He talked a little bit about the improved attendance at our games, the publicity we were getting in the local papers, the increased enthusiasm in the student body. He didn't make any effort to hide the fact that he was stroking me a little.

Then he said, "Let me tell you what I've learned. I've been

around here thirty years. You get it going really good and pretty soon, expectations are raised. That's how you get fired. What I've learned is that you should try to keep it at around five hundred [in won-lost percentage]. Don't ask the athletic department for a better field, don't ask for more money, don't ask for more scholarships. You can stay here and have a wonderful life for as long as you want. But if you start getting everyone excited and set a high standard, that's the standard you'll be judged by. And you'll have to work your tail off to meet it. Be careful."

Up until that moment, I hadn't fully realized how blessed I had been to grow up where I did, surrounded by the people who surrounded me. The coaches I'd revered in Rutland were all people who dreamed of big things and set high goals, even if, in the circumstances, winning a Vermont state championship was the highest goal they could strive for. I remember thinking, as I sat and listened to this UConn coach advise me not to raise anyone's expectations, that I didn't know there were coaches, or people who called themselves coaches, who thought this way. I promised myself that if I ever started viewing coaching the way this man did, I would quit, for the good of the kids and the good of myself—because it would really be a shame to call yourself a coach and think that way.

But as I've since learned, there are lots of people who think like that guy at UConn, though few will admit it, even to themselves. Every company has them. They're the people who have figured out how much they have to produce to make a living and hold on to their jobs. That's all they do. Even though the PGA Tour is a highly competitive environment where you have to be one of the top 125 players each season to retain your playing privileges, I see evidence of this thinking. There are players who know that if they can finish in the top ten a few times a year and make more cuts than they miss in the other events, they'll be in that top 125. That's the goal they really set for themselves, regardless of whether they'd be honest about it in a press conference.

Why would someone choose to be average, middle of the road, just a survivor? I don't think most golfers would pay a pro to teach them if the pro openly thought they were limited in their abilities and never going to be very good. But people choose to feel that way about themselves all the time. I'm not talking here about, say, a surgeon who chooses to be a mediocre, occasional golfer because he doesn't have the time to devote to the game. I know surgeons who tell me that they long ago realized they could be good surgeons, good family men, or good golfers—but just two out of three. That's the kind of surgeon I would choose for myself. I'm talking about people who choose mediocrity in one of the main pursuits of their life. They pretend that they don't have enough talent in anything to be exceptional.

I understand why people choose to do this. If you set low goals, you think you're not going to fail. Failure is painful.

I'm fortunate that people content to be average don't often ask for my time. I get to work with people whose goals and dreams excite them and excite me. When I asked LeBron James what his dreams were, he didn't hesitate. He wants to be the best basketball player of all time.

Exceptional people understand that if they set such goals,

there is no such thing as failure. If, for instance, Tiger Woods fails to match or surpass Jack Nicklaus's career totals, does that mean he's a failure? How can someone with fourteen majors be called a failure? If he doesn't get to nineteen majors, his failure will be better than the successes of all but one man. John Calipari publicly states that he wants his team to go 40-0. But if his team loses ten games and makes it to the NCAA final game, is that a failure? It's a big advantage to aim high. When you aim high, you have a chance to be great. Even your failures will be better than most people's best. I counsel people to laugh at what other people perceive as failures. I tell them not to care if other people think their goals are crazy. In fact, I tell them, if no one thinks your goals are crazy, you're probably not aiming high enough.

7.

Being Single-Minded

F OR TWO decades, I taught at the University of Virginia, which was founded by Thomas Jefferson. I live a few miles from Monticello, his home. Jefferson's influence is still strong in this environment, and one of those influences is his belief in the well-rounded individual. He himself was both a politician and a brilliant architect. He was knowledgeable about both science and the arts. When he founded the university, he determined that it would have ten departments, and he expected young men to get some knowledge in all ten. His choices reinforced an enduring tenet of American culture. To this day, I think that most Americans would say that the ideal individual should be well-rounded.

But Jefferson intended the university to serve an aristocratic, nineteenth-century class of plantation owners that doesn't exist anymore. Even in his time, I am not sure the ideal of a man who learns something about many things and pursues many interests worked all that well. Jefferson accomplished many great things, but he wasn't a particularly practical man. He died deeply in debt and his heirs had to sell Monticello. If he were alive today, I suspect he might think quite differently about how to structure a university, whether an individual should know something about many things, and how to live an exceptional life. He would recognize that in our capitalist society, the competition keeps getting tougher and the demands on a person who wants to be exceptional keep growing. That's the nature of our world.

I know that in my experience with people in both sport and business, I don't see a lot of exceptional people whom I'd characterize as well-rounded. I see a lot more people who are very single-minded. They have a passion for one thing, and they pursue it zealously. They generally reserve time for family when they're not pursuing their passion. But that's about all the spare time they have.

Some years ago, NASCAR driver Richard Petty came to see me. We talked in general for a while, and something I said about the attitude of winners caught his attention.

"Doc, you just reminded me of something about myself when I was in my prime," he said. "My mind was so good. My attitude was so good. When I got to that starting line, there was like a laser beam from the middle of my forehead to the finish line. And all I cared about was getting to that finish line first. I never got off that beam, that single-minded purpose of getting there before anyone else. Most of the drivers wanted to win. Or I should say they would have liked to win. But they also didn't want to finish last, didn't want to blow a tire and wreck the car, didn't want to look really bad. I didn't care about any of that stuff. I just wanted to get to that finish line first. And I dominated. One of the reasons I found it easy to win out there is that very few people have that laser beam, that single-minded purpose."

Richard was not the only exceptional athlete who brought up the idea of a laser to describe his focus. Pat Bradley told me that when she was on the green, she felt as if her eyes were lasers, marking the path of a putt to the hole. When she actually hit the ball, she just tried to get it on the line burned into the green by her imaginary laser. Her nephew Keegan learned this from her, and he was seeing lasers when he won the PGA Championship.

Richard Petty's and Pat Bradley's lasers appeared in actual competition, of course, but I've noticed that exceptional people tend to have a laserlike focus in nearly everything they do. I have a friend, for instance, who's very successful in real estate. We have traveled together to play golf, and he doesn't really care too much about what courses we play. He's too busy noticing the kind of development that surrounds the golf course. Real estate is his consuming interest.

Exceptional people tend not to care too much about what most people would consider "balance" in their lives. They don't allocate time equally to each aspect of their lives. Like most people, they would say their priorities are health, happiness, and success. Under the heading of happiness, like most people, they would put the quality of their relationships with family and friends. But they devote what most people would consider a disproportionate amount of time to their work, whether that work is sport or some other endeavor.

In fact, if they find that they can no longer muster that

single-minded devotion, athletes can regress. Curtis Strange, for example, was one of the best golfers in the world when he won consecutive U.S. Opens in 1988 and 1989; no one has won consecutive U.S. Opens since. He and I talked often in those days, and he fit the profile of a single-minded individual. But a year or two after that second U.S. Open, Curtis lost that single-mindedness. He has spoken of feeling relieved when the pressure of his Open streak ended. He's also spoken of feeling lethargic and depressed. Whatever it was, Curtis didn't win after that second U.S. Open. He developed other interests—he likes to hunt, to work part-time as a broadcaster, and to spend time with his wife, Sarah. In 2005, when he turned fifty, he gave the Senior Tour a try, but he acknowledged that he just didn't care that much about golf anymore and he essentially gave it up, at least competitively.

I certainly don't disagree with the choices Curtis has made in his life, and I remain an admirer of his accomplishments. But I do think his career illustrates the effect of being single-minded. I got the same impression from Ben Hogan that I had from Curtis. Hogan devoted his life to golf with a single-minded intensity until he was about fifty. That intensity enabled him to develop a remarkable golf swing without a formal instructor. It enabled him to recover from a terrible automobile wreck that seemed likely to leave him crippled. It enabled him to have perhaps the greatest golf season ever when he won the only three majors he played in 1953. But that intensity took a toll on him. It became too much. And I believe that when he realized he could no longer be single-minded, Hogan decided he no longer wanted to play golf in public. His single-mindedness was that important.

Curtis Strange and Ben Hogan shared another accomplishment that doesn't appear on their Hall of Fame plaques. They both had enduring marriages. Not all single-minded people do. Ideally, being single-minded does not mean sacrificing marriages, friends, and families. I've known many single-minded, exceptional people who had wonderful relationships with their families. But that's not always the case.

In my experience, it's critical for a single-minded person to pick the right sort of person as a spouse. Touring professional golfers need to be mindful of this. By its nature, the life of a touring player can be tough on a marriage. Spouses can and often do travel with players before children are born. This affords them the occasional free January vacation in Hawaii, which is great. But it also gives them a lot of weeks spent in a hotel in Memphis or Hartford during the heat of the summer. Moreover, the touring golfer, if he's going to be good, has to spend as many as twelve hours a day "working." He's got rounds, either in practice or in competition. He's got practice time. He's got workouts with his trainer. He may have time taken up by media requests or sponsors. Even when he's not working, he may be preoccupied with what happened on the course that day or what he wants to happen tomorrow. After the novelty of this sort of life on the road wears off, a spouse can easily begin to feel like she's a lesser priority in her husband's life—and resent it. If and when children enter the picture, the strain on the spouse can be even greater. The choice is between staying at home while the player is competing and trying to figure out day care, schooling, and meals on the road. It's not easy. Only an unusual person can pull it off.

I often counsel young golfers to be very thoughtful if they're considering getting married. It's not wise to marry someone who isn't happy if she's not the center of attention. It takes an extraordinary person to be the spouse of an exceptional person. He or she has to be unusually self-sufficient. I've seen marriages fall apart under the stress of tour life because either the husband, the wife, or both didn't really think through what they were getting into. It damages both people's lives, and it's particularly tragic when kids are involved.

Even when the marriage survives, having a parent who is driven to be exceptionally successful can be rough on the children. Unlike the spouse, the kids didn't choose to be in a family with someone who's driven to succeed. It can be tough for a child who feels the need for parental attention to hear, over and over, that Mom is at the office or Dad is at the stadium watching game film. There is no shortage of children of famously successful people who will testify that their very successful parent was less than successful at home.

The people I know who manage to be great at both their careers and their family lives are either very fortunate, very admirable, or both. It is possible to have both. You must make a happy marriage and a happy family part of your definition of success rather than seeing the marriage and the family as an obligation or encumbrance. But you need a spouse who understands and supports your drive to succeed. Jack Nicklaus is legendary for having the greatest career in golf history and at the same time running a business and raising five kids who, in adulthood, all choose to live close to their parents' home. But a large share of the credit for that belongs to Barbara Nicklaus, whom he married at the age of twenty. She is as exceptional in the business of being a wife and mother as Jack was at playing golf.

You may need to come up with your own definition of what "having it all" means. I read the debates about whether women can "have it all." To my mind, the question can apply equally to men. And in my view, if by "having it all" you mean having an exceptional career and simultaneously spending one day a week as a volunteer parent in your child's class-room, and being an amateur triathlete, you can't have it all. There aren't enough hours in the day or week. You have to figure out a way to make the time you spend with your family and the time you spend at work both extremely efficient and effective. You have to accept that you'll give less than your best effort to some nonessentials. It's not easy. There is no single formula that will work for every case, all the time.

Given the potential costs of a single-minded drive to be exceptional, I don't think that most people choose to be that way. It happens. It rises from their passion to do something as well as they possibly can, the way Richard Petty wanted to win NASCAR races and Pat Bradley wanted to win golf tourna-ments. It takes root in their lives because it works.

People who are single-minded perceive their labor differ-ently than most people. If you ask an average person to work a twelve-hour day, he's likely to feel overworked. As the hours go on, the average person is going to think more and more about the dinner at home he's not having, about the TV he's not watching, about the beer he's not drinking. If you ask the average person after a twelve-hour shift how he feels, he's likely to say he's exhausted. But the single-minded person is likely not to have noticed how many hours went by.

The single-minded person isn't distracted by things like television, beers with the boys, or even dinner at home. He's engrossed in what he's doing. He's fascinated by it. The hours go by and he doesn't feel tired. He may even feel exhilarated by the opportunity to do what he loves doing.

I heard a story from Brad Faxon recently that illustrates the way champions are single-minded. Brad is a New Englander and a big fan of all the New England teams, including the Patriots. He's become friends with Tom Brady. A couple of years ago, New England pulled out a big win against San Diego in the final minutes. On the day after the win, Brad called Brady.

"Congratulations. What a great win!" Brad said. "Man, that must've been some party on the flight home."

"Brad, we have a no-drinking policy on our flights," Brady said. "By the time we got on the plane in San Diego, every player had a computer at his seat with next week's opponent broken down position by position. That flight home is the best five hours we're going to get to prepare for next week. Monday will be taken up with a lot of physical rehab. Tuesday is taken up with a lot of PR and endorsement stuff. If we waited until Wednesday to start getting ready for next week, we'd have already lost. There wouldn't be enough time."

That's what single-mindedness looks like on a team level.

There's no extended celebrating, no distraction, while there is a need to prepare. Preparation time is too precious.

This pays off in performance. The single-minded person puts in the time required to meet his high standards. Maybe that standard is a 4.0 average in school. Maybe it's leading a pro football team into the playoffs. Maybe it's an Olympic medal. For most endeavors, there's a high correlation between the work that goes in and the results that come out. (It's not a perfect correlation, which I'll get into in another chapter.) To some people, looking from the outside, the single-minded person can seem obsessed. Looking at himself in the mirror, the single-minded person sees someone doing what he wants to do and needs to do to succeed.

There no doubt can be a bit of cultural distortion in the way someone perceives single-minded effort. An American kid who wants to be great at golf and practices three hours a day is likely to be lauded by all who know him as a very hard worker. That's because in the context of an American country club, he is. I'm not an expert on Asian cultures, but I have seen enough Korean golfers to know that in Korea, a competitive golfer who practiced three hours a day would likely be considered a slacker. If a Korean kid decides she wants to excel at golf, the hours she devotes to golf will dwarf those spent by the corresponding American. Many American parents would blanch at the idea of a child spending six or eight hours a day practicing golf. They'd be fearful that the child was devoting too much time to golf at the expense of other things. It seems to me that this view is a bit of American cultural astigmatism, brought about by decades of movies and television shows.

These movies and television shows conveyed the idea that the proper American childhood and adolescence had time for some studying, yes, but also for music lessons and choir practice, for sports, for tuning up a hot rod, for sitting in a tree house gazing at the sky, and for going to the malt shop after school to share a shake with the pretty girl in algebra class. That may have been true when Mickey Rooney and Judy Garland were young, but I don't think it's true in the modern world. The money lists on both the men's and women's golf tours show that competition is coming from all over the world now, and it's tougher than ever to be the best.

I have clients who are single-minded, and many of them are very successful. I find myself on occasion cautioning them to take their foot off the accelerator once in a while. Padraig Harrington, for instance, is a driven golfer. He takes care to pay attention to his family and his friends, and he's one of the most affable people I know. But there is no mistaking the fact that he is single-minded in his pursuit of the best golf he can play. Sometimes it hurts him. He's always been willing to work very hard to improve his golf swing, for instance. I try to tell him that he's reached the point where his golf swing is fine. He doesn't need to keep tinkering with it. He knows how to hit the ball. I'm glad he worked as hard as he worked to get that swing. Now it's time to think about being fresh and rested when he competes, rather than beating balls all day on the range just before a tournament. I try to remind him that they don't give the trophy to the person who's hit the most practice balls. But it's hard for Padraig to take that advice. It takes more discipline for him not to practice than it takes for him to practice. Because he is so exceptional, he listens to people he trusts and works to change his behavior, taking the time to rest, trusting his golf swing. That paid off for him late in 2014, when he rested the week before the Indonesia Open on the Asian Tour, then won the tournament. In fact, the weather in Jakarta that week helped him, because it turned the practice range into a quagmire that was all but unusable. Instead of working hard on his swing and fretting about it, as he sometimes does, Padraig could only do a few one-handed drills. He played the tournament with no expectations or pre-conceptions about his ball-striking, deciding that all he could do was keep a smile on his face and focus his mind on his targets. That's not a bad attitude to have in competition.

So I understand that simply being single-minded is not always the answer. On the other hand, Padraig's intensity has led him to three major championships and a great deal of money. Given the choice between being single-minded and casual in your commitment, I'd take single-minded every time.

8.

Learned Effectiveness:
The Virtuous Circle

W HEN I was in graduate school, one of the most influential voices in American psychology was Martin Seligman of the University of Pennsylvania. He was a cognitive psychologist, and that was the branch of the discipline to which I was instinctively attracted. Cognitive psychology, to put it simply, believes that human beings can control the condition of their psyches by using their conscious brains to monitor and change the way they think. Cognitive psychologists are the heirs of William James and his belief that people tend to become what they think of themselves. They carved out a way of treating people that was distinctly different from Freudianism, the dominant therapeutic approach of the middle of the last century. Freud believed that people are essentially the products of their instincts and their upbringing. Cognitive psychology gave a more central role to the conscious mind and the human will.

Seligman was interested in helping people suffering from

depression. He and his associates conducted experiments, largely on animals, that led to their theory of "learned helplessness." In their experiments, they subjected dogs to a series of mild, unavoidable shocks. Then they changed the structure of the experiments so the dogs had a way of avoiding the shocks if they could figure it out and use it. They found that many dogs didn't use the escape mechanism. These dogs, after suffering a series of shocks, had "learned" that they were helpless. Seligman saw a parallel to humans who suffered from chronic depression. These people had "learned" that when something bad happened to them, there was nothing they could do to recover. Their thoughts about themselves ran to this sort of statement: "I flunked my math test. I'm stupid and I'll never get it. I might as well drop out." Seligman's work led to treatments for depression that concentrated on helping the patient identify these sorts of thoughts, catch them, and replace them with more helpful ones: "I flunked my math test. I need to study more and get some tutoring, and if I do I can pass the next one."

The truly sad aspect of Seligman's work on learned helplessness was something that William James could have predicted—many people were becoming what they thought about themselves. A depressed person might react to a social setback by thinking there was something fundamentally unattractive about him, that normal people would not want to be near him. And that would ultimately prove to be true. But if you interviewed the associates of this person, you would find that they didn't think he was inherently unattractive or unpleasant. It was just that his depressing view of himself and the world inevitably emerged in his interactions with other people. They would say that they didn't want to associate with him because he was always complaining, always criticizing.

Though I admired the insights that Seligman brought to his work, I wasn't interested in helplessness. I was interested in the exceptional. As I worked with athletes and other people striving to be exceptional, I found that no matter what happened to them, no matter what setbacks occurred in their lives, they found causes to keep trying. They always sought and discovered a reason to believe in themselves. A fundamental factor in their exceptionality was the way they perceived and reacted to the events in their lives.

Let's suppose that you were a member of a football team that had won two games and lost nine going into the final game of the season. I've worked with such teams. A lot of players on this losing team might decide, whether they'd admit it or not, that there was no hope. They'd conclude from the evidence of the first eleven games that they were no good—not big enough, not fast enough, not talented enough. They would have, in Seligman's terms, learned helplessness. But a certain number of the players on this beleaguered team would perceive things differently. They'd focus on ways the team had improved during the year, even if the record didn't show it. They'd reflect on plays that had worked. They'd believe in their ability to correct mistakes made during plays that hadn't worked. These players would play well during that twelfth game. If a team had enough of these players, it might well pull an upset. These players had the character traits of exceptional people.

Working with such people, I developed and taught a theory I called "learned effectiveness." It's almost the opposite side of the coin that Seligman called learned helplessness. (Seligman himself started to think and write along similar lines. His best-known book is now a 1990 work called *Learned Optimism*.)

Learned effectiveness flows from the character traits we've been talking about—optimism, confidence, respect for your own talent, persistence, and commitment. There's a certain chicken-and-egg problem that can arise here. What comes first—effectiveness and achievement, or confidence, optimism, and belief in yourself? Some people I see would like to argue with me and say that they're naturally pessimistic and uncertain, and they can't change those traits without first achieving success. I don't buy that. I know from experience that people can teach themselves to be confident and optimistic, then use those traits to help them achieve success.

I believe that rather than worry about the chicken-and-egg question, it's more helpful to think of a virtuous circle at work in the minds of exceptional people. They have optimism and confidence. Because they are optimistic and confident, they react to setbacks not by getting discouraged and giving up, but with persistence. Their attitude is, "I'm not playing well right now, but when I put it all together [or *our team* puts it all together], I'll really be something. I can beat anybody." Because they persist, they get better. Because they get better, they experience success. And that success reinforces their optimism, their confidence, and their respect for their own talent. That's the virtuous circle.

I see the impact of learned effectiveness on the golf course. Certain players, if they warm up poorly or mishit a few shots on the opening holes, go into a funk. They think, "I haven't got it today. My swing is off. I need to finish this tournament, see my teacher, and fix my swing." Or they decide that they're just not making any putts, and they reconcile themselves to shooting a 76 and missing the cut.

In contrast, a golfer who has learned effectiveness will react to a poor range session or a few early mishits by thinking, "Okay, this is a day where my short game and my course management are going to really help me. No matter where I hit it, I can find a way to get the ball in the hole and post a good score." Maybe they stop hitting their balky drivers and play an iron from a lot of tees, just to keep the ball in play. Maybe they just see themselves as players who always shoot par or better and figure that if their long swing is off, it just means that their putting will be particularly sharp. There is no single way of thinking. But there is a common element in the way players who have learned effectiveness react to a day when their games are off. They're optimistic rather than pessimistic. They're confident rather than uncertain about themselves. When they miss a green, they're looking to pitch the ball into the hole rather than worried about not getting up and down. They're constantly looking for good breaks.

Of course, golfers who have learned effectiveness occasionally shoot 79 despite their attitudes. But let's say that golfers have their best physical stuff 50 percent of the time and are less than their best the other 50 percent. Over the course of a season, the players who have learned effectiveness are going to battle through their swing issues far more often than those who are dependent on feeling that they're in a groove to play well. That translates into many more cuts made and many more dollars earned. They believe that they can play good golf even when their swings are off because they are confident about their minds.

And when their games are right, players with learned effectiveness tend to take better advantage. They've learned to love their great days more than they hate their bad days and to hold on to them in their memories longer. They live for their great putts, their great shots, their great rounds, and their wins. They build on their successes. In contrast, players who don't have the attributes of learned effectiveness tend to play not to lose badly. They worry about having a bad run, a bad year, and losing their cards. Even when they win or play well, they wake up the next morning thinking about the flaws in their game and worried about whether they're going to play well or win again.

People who have learned effectiveness have a filter that sifts out the comments from other people that will help them and allows the unhelpful comments to fall away without affecting them. You can see this in schools. Kids these days probably hear negative comments from their teachers less often than they did when I was growing up. Teachers today have been trained not to discourage their students. Yet there are still lots of comments and evaluations a child can choose to ignore or take to heart. Kids get cut from teams or stuck on the bench. Kids get steered from one track to another in school, even if the school no longer uses the term "track." If a child hears a guidance counselor say, "I wouldn't recommend AP English for you. Maybe shop would be a better choice," the kid can react in one of two ways. He can accept the suggestion that he take shop and decide that the counselor must know what he's talking about, that he's not very smart and he'll never learn anything, never succeed in college, and he might as well stop studying and enjoy his evenings. Or he can decide that the counselor isn't a very good judge of talent and he's going to take AP despite him, he's going to get a great education, and he's going to wind up smarter than the counselor. People who have learned effectiveness often like a little chip on their shoulders.

Conversely, people who have learned effectiveness latch on to any positive input that comes their way and feed on it.

I know a young woman who came to the United States from Cameroon when she was seventeen, speaking almost no English. She was bright, but her circumstances were daunting. She was placed in an ESOL class for her first year in an American public school. She got into a regular English class for her senior year. In the first few weeks of that class, her teacher casually asked her how long she had been in the United States.

"Eighteen months," she replied.

"You speak English very well for someone here only eighteen months," the teacher said before moving on with the lesson.

The young woman chose to make that offhand comment very meaningful in her life. She let it encourage her to believe that she had a chance to excel in her last year in public school and win a scholarship that would enable her to go to college. Four years later, having done precisely that, she graduated magna cum laude with a degree in biology, eager to pursue a career in medicine.

She climbed onto the virtuous circle. Her response to a simple sentence from her teacher restored a piece of the confidence and optimism she'd grown up with in Africa. She used that confidence to get good grades and earn a scholarship. She worked hard. She grew more optimistic and more confident as her academic laurels mounted. She worked even harder. That's the way learned effectiveness works. Winning breeds success.

As I've said, learned effectiveness doesn't always spill over from one area of a person's life to another. Just because someone is a successful athlete, for instance, doesn't mean that he'll be successful in a business career he undertakes after his playing career is over. But it's very advisable to have that virtuous circle working for you in the primary endeavors of your life. It's even more advisable to learn to transfer learned effectiveness skills to every effort that you care about. Without learned effectiveness, it's very hard to succeed.

9.

Nerves and the Performance Process

EOPLE WITH a superficial knowledge of my work tend to think I cure cases of nervousness. They're wrong.

Nerves are, in fact, a big part of what I deal with when I counsel golfers, other athletes, businesspeople, or people in any field that demands performance. But there's no cure for nerves.

Every one of the golfers I've counseled who have won major championships has been nervous during the final holes of these tournaments. But they've learned to perform well despite nerves and the physical symptoms that accompany them—trembling, wet hands, rapid heartbeat, a sinking feeling in the gut, and sometimes even a feeling that breathing is difficult.

These physical symptoms of nerves are the products of inevitable chemical changes that occur inside the body during moments of high stress, changes like a shot of adrenaline.

They're outside our conscious control. So it's a waste of time trying to avoid them.

To underscore this point, I sometimes ask clients whether they remember their first kiss. Invariably, they do. Then I ask whether they were nervous just before the big moment.

"Yeah, I was shaking like a leaf" is a common response.

And did being nervous ruin the experience?

Upon reflection, most people say no. They decide that being nervous enhanced the experience and made it more significant and memorable.

Nerves are in fact a sign that an individual is about to do something he cares deeply about, whether it's a first kiss, a first major championship, or a big performance in front of the public.

Jimmie Johnson has won six NASCAR Sprint Cup championships as I write this, and by the time you read it, there's a very good chance he'll have won seven or more. Yet Jimmie once came to me and asked, "What if I told you that on the night before a race I am scared to death that I'm going to get in the car and totally forget how to drive a race car?"

"Have you ever gotten in the car and forgotten how to drive it?" I asked.

"Nope," he said.

"Then I guess it doesn't matter," I told him. "I guess it's just how you get ready."

"That's it?" he asked me, a little surprised that I would dismiss his thoughts so easily.

But that was it. I told Jimmie that a lot of athletes and

performers use worry and fear as a cue or a spur to help them prepare for a big event. They make nerves work for them. Bill Russell used to vomit before every NBA game. Then he'd play great basketball. He won eleven NBA championships.

It would have been another story if Jimmie had told me that his nerves caused him to take to his bed for days at a time and therefore fail to prepare. But they didn't. He simply used them as a reminder to make sure he thought through his strategy and visualized the upcoming race. Once the flag dropped and the car accelerated, he forgot them. (And he remembered how to drive.)

Sometimes the prospect of making big money causes an athlete or performer to find himself blocked by nerves. Players on major team sports can encounter this when they sign multimillion-dollar contracts and suddenly must prove they're worth that much money. Performers can face analogous challenges. I've worked in recent years with John Rzeznik, the guitarist and songwriter for the Goo Goo Dolls. When he came to me, John and the band had made several albums and toured the world. But because of the way their first recording contracts were structured, they didn't have much money to show for it. Their financial future was heavily dependent on the success of a new album they had yet to make, their first with Warner Bros. Records. With millions of dollars on the line, John sat down to write—and couldn't. He was too nervous. He was blocked.

I couldn't make light of John's nervous block, the way I'd done with Jimmie Johnson's fears, because, like me, John had been raised in modest circumstances, and there was no way for him to make light of millions of dollars. It was just too much money. And I don't know anything about writing songs.

But I do know that when an athlete or a performer in fact has the skills and talent to succeed, he doesn't need to let his nerves get in the way. John had talent, and he'd worked hard to develop and polish it. He was like a golfer who has the skills to play great but needs to get out of his own way to play his best under pressure.

To do that, he needed to develop and rely on a process. I've talked already about one kind of process, the preparation process. That's the practice routine that individuals and teams follow as they get ready for competition. It's what John Calipari calls "the grind." The preparation process is an absolutely essential part of success. But when it's time to compete or to perform, champions lean on another sort of process, the performance process.

You'll remember that I suggested to LeBron James that if he wanted to become a better three-point shooter, he needed to start by committing himself to making two hundred three-point shots off the dribble and two hundred catch-and-shoot three-point shots every day in practice. That's a preparation process. LeBron's performance process for shooting three-pointers might be very simple—just a matter of seeing the basket and reacting to it without thinking about his shooting mechanics or the outcome. There's not much time, in a basketball game, for anything else.

For a golfer, the performance process is more complex, because there's a lot more time to think between golf shots and the golfer isn't reacting to what other players do. (Or he shouldn't be. He should be playing the course.) A golfer's performance process is a preshot routine that's designed to put his mind and body into the proper places every time he makes a shot in a tournament. A good preshot routine is both mental and physical. The player clears his mind and forgets about his last shot and all previous and future shots. There is only the shot to be played. There is only the present moment. He doesn't think about the consequences of the shot or about the way it will affect the results of the tournament. He doesn't try to conduct a one-person, internal seminar on positive thinking. He only knows he will accept the shot he is about to hit, find the ball, and go through the same routine for the next shot. He visualizes the shot that he wants to hit and makes all the necessary judgments about the club to use, the wind, the break of the green, and any other factors that might affect it. Then—and this can be the hard part—he trusts that his body can execute the shot. He turns off the conscious brain. He lets the subconscious—where the best control of fine motor skills can be found—govern his movements. He looks at the target, looks at the ball, and swings. He hits the shot without consciously trying to control his body. He plays instinctively, athletically.

Nervousness can disrupt all this. Nervousness prods the conscious brain to keep control of the proceedings because of fear. The performer is afraid that he'll mishit a shot and humiliate himself on television or miss the cut and lose his playing privileges. If he succumbs to nervousness, he'll let his conscious brain have control. As a result, he'll swing without his normal grace and rhythm. He'll probably mishit the shot. The performer needs to learn to see nerves as a friend that will help him perform at a high level. Great performers train themselves to have quieter minds as their bodies get excited because they in fact do see nerves as a friend. Just as a visit by a good friend can relax and soothe you in a stressful time, the onset of nerves relaxes them.

The golfer needs to find a way to trust his ability in these circumstances, and a preshot routine enables him to do that. It calms him. Its mental subtext, if you will, is that this is just another shot, like hundreds of thousands of shots he's hit in practice and in games, using this same preshot routine or performance process. That's what Rory McIlroy was talking about when he spoke after winning the 2014 British Open. He said he went through the final round trying to think of only two words: "process" and "spot." ("Spot" was a reference to the point he wanted to roll his ball over as he putted, so it was really a variation on the idea of process, applied to putting.) Rory has learned that the way to win majors is to trust in his performance process. For full shots, that meant looking at the target and letting the ball go to the target. For putts, it meant looking at the spot and rolling the ball to the spot, trusting that it would do as he wanted.

I should note that I rarely use the word "trust" with a player without also using the word "train." The mantra is "train it and trust it." If I had to go out onstage with the Goo Goo Dolls and perform in front of a big crowd using only the very rusty clarinet skills I learned in the ninth grade in Rutland, I'd be nervous and there wouldn't be much I could do about it. I wouldn't have any training or skills to trust. A good performance process wouldn't help me. There is no substitute for acquiring and polishing skills through practice.

But when someone does have the talent and has trained himself, a performance process can enable him to work around the nerves that are getting in his way. In John Rzeznik's case, the process of writing songs was a mental one. John has a tremendous ability to express human feelings in lyrics. He had to let go of his fear and doubt. His nervous block amounted to worry that he'd written all his good songs already and not made any money from them, that people wouldn't like the new ones, that they wouldn't be any good. I had to help him find a process to get past that. I just turned on a tape recorder and asked him to start talking about his life and himself. He did. And as he talked, I could hear songs. I sat there listening and saying to myself, "Yep, that's a great song. Yep, that's another one." John just needed a process that let him stop worrying about the outcome of his labor and immerse himself in what he does best. As he talked to me, he stopped worrying about what others would think, stopped judging what he was saying, stopped evaluating what he was saying. That process worked. He got the song concepts and a lot of the lyrics for the entire album in about two days of talking. That album became *Dizzy Up the Girl*. It went triple platinum. John sent me a copy of the platinum record and it hangs on the wall in my basement, where I work with clients, amid the assortment of pin flags and golf magazine covers, baseballs, basketballs, and NASCAR memorabilia that come from my more typical encounters.

This principle applies to golfers. I remember working with a very gifted golfer some years ago. It was early in his PGA Tour career. This golfer had a lot of success in the junior and collegiate ranks. He spent a year or so on what was then called the Nike Tour, and then he rose to the PGA Tour. He soon got frustrated because he didn't immediately win there.

We talked about it. "Doc, if I could ever play in a tournament the way I play in pro-ams or when I'm home with friends, I'd be winning," he said. I asked him what he thought about when he was with friends or in a pro-am. The answer was not much.

"In a pro-am, I walk up to every tee box. I pull my driver unless it's a dogleg where I might hit it through the fairway. I look at my target, I see my trajectory, and I hit it. I never think about what's right or left of the fairway. It's not even a factor. Then I get to my ball in the fairway, and the caddie says one hundred fifty yards or whatever. I grab a club, I look at the target, I see a trajectory, and I hit it. I walk up to the green and I talk to the guys I'm playing with as we walk. And I can see what my putt's going to do as I'm walking onto the green. I don't ever walk around or work hard to read my putts, because I already know what they're going to do, and I make putts from everywhere.

"But when I get in a tournament, Doc, every shot starts a discussion. I'll be on the tee, and I'll be asking my caddie, 'Do you think it's a driver? A three-wood? A one-iron?' I start to think I don't want to make any dumb mistakes. By the time I finally look at the target and see my ball flight, I've put just enough crap in my head about what I don't want to do that

I can't possibly swing as freely as I swing when I'm just seeing it and doing it. If I'm out on the fairway and the caddie says one hundred fifty pin, I pull the eight-iron and then I start to think. I put the eight-iron back and I look at my caddie and say, 'Well, do you think it's a big nine? A smooth eight? Or a little seven? I don't know. Throw up some grass.' So he throws up the grass and I go, 'Geez. Throw it up where there's some breeze, will you?' So I got him throwing grass up two or three times because he didn't throw it high enough the first time. And then it's, 'Well, what is it to clear the front bunker? How far to the front edge of the back bunker?' And then it's, 'Well, what [hazards] do we want to miss here?' By the time I finally make up my mind again, I've turned on my conscious brain enough that it's just not as free and flowing. It's like I'm playing not to make a mistake instead of to play great. I'm just not turning it over to my subconscious and my instinct."

This player didn't need my help to figure out what he was doing wrong. He already knew it. He'd just explained it to me as well as any of my grad students could have done. His nervousness in PGA Tour events caused him to abandon the very effective, simple preshot routine, or performance process, he used when he was playing with friends. Because he was nervous, he rethought and overthought the decisions a golfer must make before every shot—how far to hit it, what club to use, and so forth. As he said, he turned on his conscious brain. I always counsel golfers to strive to keep the conscious brain out of their golf games when they're in competition. The only thing I want the player in competition to do with his conscious brain is figure out the route from his hotel to the golf course. The subconscious should handle everything after that.

Of course, the trick is not so much knowing how to think; it's thinking that way under pressure. It would be simpler, in a way, if my client were, say, a pro football cornerback. Once a play started, he wouldn't have much time to think. He'd look for the keys his defensive coordinator had told him to look for and react instantly. But most situations are not like that. We have time to think, whether our task is making a pitch shot or making a sales call.

I told this young golfer that he needed to be willing to take risks. He needed to commit himself to going with his first instincts when he picked a club, selected a target, or read a putt. That first instinct is the product of the subconscious brain, and he had honed his subconscious perception over thousands of practice shots and rounds of golf. The first instinct of an experienced golfer, I've found, is usually correct. Even if it's wrong, swinging decisively, with a clear mind, will almost always turn out better than swinging with a mind cluttered by conscious thoughts. Yes, it was possible he would ignore some factor if he went with his first instincts. Yes, it was possible he'd hit through a fairway or reach a bunker if he went with his driver. Yes, it was possible he'd pick the wrong club for his approach to the green and wind up in a bunker. But so what? He knew how to hit from the rough and the sand. And any round of golf is going to contain at least a few errors. The risks of playing with his first judgments were manageable. The benefits were enormous.

My advice didn't lead to an overnight change. Like most

things, the way a player thinks on a golf course is in part a question of habit. My client had to spend time developing better thinking habits. He had to learn to quiet his conscious brain and not think when he was nervous. He had to shut the conscious brain down and let the subconscious system take over. But he did. And the changes paid off. He started to win tournaments.

It's helpful to think of an effective performance process as a good habit, particularly when an individual has made thinking poorly a bad habit. We understand that it takes many repetitions over an indefinite period of time to build a good habit. That kind of purposeful repetition is often required to build a good performance process. It's usually not something that an individual can read or hear, agree with, and put into perfect operation right away. Progress occasionally comes quickly, but it isn't always consistent, steady progress leading to a durable result. There can be fits and starts.

I started working with Jim Furyk just before the 2013 PGA Championship at Oak Hill in Rochester. He was unhappy with his recent performance and told me he was not enjoying himself as much as he had in the past. He was fighting his putting, particularly on the shorter putts. As we talked about it, it became clear to both of us that on short putts, Jim had fallen into the bad habit of thinking about his stroke; thinking about technique is not something you want to do during a performance process. We understood that the cure was not to think, "Don't think about your stroke," as he started to putt. The subconscious often doesn't understand the word "don't." If Jim tried to fix his problem by telling himself not to think about his stroke, he would most likely have turned on his conscious brain and prompted it to think about the stroke—precisely what he was trying to avoid. The solution was to build a new, good habit that would displace the bad one.

Jim, of course, already had a putting routine. We worked on strengthening it, especially on strengthening the last moments when he needed to focus on his target and stroke the ball without conscious thought. Jim likes to walk up to the ball and address it, try to see the line, then walk behind the ball and read it again. He does this to prevent ambivalence. He doesn't want to read the putt from behind the ball, then walk up, address the ball, and think that he's seeing something slightly different. That can lead to an indecisive stroke. He understands the importance of being decisive, and his routine is designed to give him clarity and certainty.

We talked about the line he envisioned as he went through this process. I often advise golfers to get themselves a chalk line, a builder's tool that can be used to lay a faint, straight line in chalk dust, extending from a hole on a level part of a practice putting green to a point from five to ten feet away. (The line will be washed away the next time the green is watered.) The player practices rolling putts along the line and into the hole. It's helpful in several ways. It helps the player feel confident that he can roll the ball along the line he wants. It helps him focus on his target rather than his stroke. It builds confidence, because he'll see a lot of balls roll into the hole. And it usually isn't too long before he starts "seeing" a line to the hole when he putts in competition. Jim preferred a similar practice aid, a string that he stretched from the hole to a point seven or eight feet away, with enough air underneath it to allow his putter blade and the ball to move back and forth. He liked seeing the putter blade move back and forth under the string and seeing the ball roll along the string line into the hole. That was fine. We had to work a little bit to make sure Jim didn't get too perfectionistic about making the ball roll precisely under the string. I reminded him that the hole was a lot wider than the string.

In order to make the revised routine a habit, I suggested to Jim that for the following three months, he go to the practice green with only one ball and follow his entire routine for every practice putt. Jim committed to doing that, and I know that Jim spends a lot of time on the practice putting green. Most players go to the putting green with several balls and they roll one after another without taking time to go through their entire routine. Jim was going to look different. He didn't care. He put the highlights of his routine in a text he kept on his phone so he could read it whenever he practiced.

Jim's putted very well since he made these changes, but it's still a work in progress. We sometimes evaluate and refine the new habit. We talk about whether he sees the line he draws on his ball rolling straight as the ball rolls; that's one of the visual clues he uses to monitor his putting. We talk about his priorities. Jim wants to feel that adhering to his performance process is the first priority, with the outcome of each putt secondary. The performance process is what he can control. A lot of outside factors, such as the condition of the green, can influence whether the ball goes in the hole.

Of course, when you adhere to a sound performance

process, the results tend to take care of themselves. Jim has worked hard on playing without expectations and being patient. He wants to accept whatever happens on the golf course and not let it affect him as he plays—whether it's a birdie or a bogey. He's emphasized playing his own game against himself and the golf course and enjoying the challenge of doing this every day. In addition, he's prioritized taking lots of time off to enjoy being with his wife and children. In essence, he is learning that you can have a life and be a great golfer, given his many previous years of dedication.

In 2014, at the age of forty-four, Jim finished fourth in the FedExCup standings. He made the cut in every tournament he entered, an indicator of great consistency. He led the Tour the entire year in scrambling percentage and almost broke the all-time record for this statistic. He didn't win a tournament, but he won the battle with himself by consistently imposing his will on his routine. He has tremendous peace of mind. People who understand the game appreciate what Jim is doing. He ranks fourth on the all-time PGA Tour money list with sixteen wins and a U.S. Open, plus numerous appearances on Ryder Cup and Presidents Cup teams.

I often encounter a misapprehension among my clients about focus and the performance process. If I told them the story I've just told you, they'd likely imagine Jim Furyk grinding his teeth during his putting routine, his brow furrowed with the strain of concentration. They'd associate what he was doing with hoary old sports terms like "bearing down" and "working hard" to stay focused on his line instead of his stroke. In fact, the opposite is usually true. The point of a performance process in sports is to remove the mental barriers that prevent a player from letting his subconscious govern his movements, prevent him from what I call "freeing it up and letting it go." When a player can't do this, I talk to him about "getting out of his own way." When he's doing it, we talking about "trying softer" or "being in the zone," or "letting it happen instead of making it happen."

Individuals get to this desired state in many ways, though I've never encountered anyone who did it by grinding his teeth and trying to force himself. I have a young client named Chris Hickman whom I started working with when he was in high school. He wasn't considered a great junior player and he wasn't recruited by any of the colleges in the powerhouse conferences. He had clear potential, but he often seemed to get in his own way during competition.

Then, this past summer, Chris blossomed. He won the Delaware open and amateur championships. Then he went to the Eastern Amateur championship, opened with a 61, and won by eight strokes, finishing at twenty-two under par. He showed well in the Porter Cup, which was his first taste of elite, national amateur competition, with a 66 in the final round. People started noticing him and how well he was playing.

Chris stopped by to talk and I congratulated him on his accomplishments. I asked him what had changed.

"Well, you told me that if I found myself getting in my own way, I should take my mind wherever as I walked between shots, then bring it back to the game when I started my preshot routine," he said. "So in the state open, I started imagining myself in a Paris café where I was invisible and I could just watch the people on the sidewalk. I started making everything."

He looked at me a little apprehensively. "What do you think?" he asked.

"Awesome," I said.

Later that summer, Chris went on, his between-shot daydreams took a more romantic turn. In the Eastern Amateur, he daydreamed about a girl he had a secret crush on. They were walking on a beach in Monaco (Chris has never been to either Paris or Monaco), having a good time, smiling. In his next tournament, he daydreamed about a girl he'd met when she was driving the beverage cart at a course he played. In the daydream, she told him she liked him and wouldn't care if he lost or won. He started taking aim at flags with his wedges and seeing putts fall. He won.

I mentioned what Chris had told me to some of the professionals I work with and found that it resonated with them. Charl Schwartzel, the 2011 Masters champion, told me his place of peace is his ranch in South Africa. He "goes there" while walking between shots, imagining himself playing with his children. When he can get himself into this reverie before he starts his preshot routine, it helps him see his shots and let his swing happen without conscious control. In fact, he shot a five-under-par 67 in the final round of the British Open the day after we talked about this. I recalled that some years ago, Chip Beck shot a 59, one of the first in the history of the PGA Tour. He told me that between shots during that round, he thought about the foundation he'd established to provide scholarships to deserving, needy students. For Chip, those thoughts removed the burden of pressure from him and depersonalized the experience. When he got to his ball and went into his preshot routine, he performed almost flawlessly. I've been told by other players that they distract themselves by concentrating on their breathing or counting the different species of trees they see on the course, even thinking about someone ill or handicapped. They'll resort to almost anything to avoid letting their thoughts drift toward the outcome of the round or the results they expect. Thoughts about outcomes and results come from the conscious brain, and they want to keep the conscious brain quiet, almost inactive. They want their subconscious to be unimpeded when they begin their preshot routines.

But they may not want to tell folks about it. The next time I saw Chris, he was on his way back to school, and he dropped by. I had another young player in my basement at the time, but I wanted this player to hear what Chris had figured out about getting out of his own way and letting go of conscious control during his performance process.

Chris looked at the floor. "Oh, I was just doing a lot of stupid stuff."

"Whoa," I said. "Why would you call it stupid if it worked for you?"

Chris opened up a bit and talked about his actual golf course daydreams.

The other player in the room exclaimed, "That reminds me of stuff I've thought about when I've played great!"

Chris was relieved by this affirmation. But I didn't advise

him to start telling everyone about the way he'd found to improve his performance process and get out of his own way. It probably wouldn't work for everyone. Individuals need to find their own paths to the state Chris had reached. And I certainly wouldn't advise a professional to start talking to the media about his between-shot daydreams, whether they involved a ranch in South Africa or a pretty girl in the gallery. People wouldn't understand the context, and the media are still in thrall to the "grit your teeth and bear down" model of focus during performance. They'd roast someone who told them about his daydreams and then, at some future point, faltered in performance.

Letting go of fear and conscious control is not easy under the best of circumstances, in part because the habit of conscious thought is drilled into us at an early age. Think of the teachers who told you in grade school to pay attention and work carefully. We're taught in school to have faith in conscious control. And it may be that on certain kinds of math tests, or in certain kinds of science experiments, conscious control is the best way to proceed. But it's not in athletics. It's not in many endeavors. I've spoken of surgeons who listen to music and chat about many things while they operate. It helps them let go of their fears about the consequences if the surgery doesn't work. My dad, working as a barber, liked to chat with his customers about whatever interested them. He did that partly because they liked the conversation, but he also understood that keeping his conscious brain out of the process of cutting hair allowed him to do his best work. Surgery and barbering, of course, were the same profession centuries ago. They both involve motor skills.

But I see the same principle at work in endeavors that involve no motor skills. Archimedes discovered the principle of buoyancy not by sitting at a desk and pondering but by getting into a hot bath, presumably a moment when his conscious brain relaxed and his subconscious was free to work. That particular "Eureka!" moment may be a myth, but we have plenty of other accounts by scientists of how important ideas came to them when they were *not* consciously seeking them. Financial analysts and consultants, if they've worked long and hard to learn their business, develop what they think of as a "gut" for knowing when to sell and when to buy. I want my financial adviser to be experienced and prudent, of course. But I also want her to trust that gut feeling when she suggests investments. If I had an illness, I would of course want my doctor to engage in a thorough and appropriate process before diagnosing me. But during that process, I would not want him to be paralyzed by doubts and fears about what might happen to me. I'd want him to trust in the process. I would want him to stop worrying about the outcome.

That's a lesson most of the great coaches emphasize. Nick Saban at Alabama is one of them. Nick preaches process every day in practice. He tells his players that Alabama football players don't think about championships. They think about and execute their processes, both in preparation and in performance. The championships come. Doc Rivers, when he coached the Boston Celtics, told his players not to worry about the scoreboard. He just wanted them to execute on both ends of the floor. He would take care of worrying about the score. He coached the Celtics to an NBA title in 2008. Florida State football coach Jimbo Fisher believes in much the same thing. Prior to the 2014 ACC Championship game, the broadcast moved into his locker room. He told his players not to let their nerves cause them think about the outcome or the score during the game. He told them to think about their assignments on the upcoming play. Florida State won.

I've helped Merrill Lynch train financial consultants to handle sales calls. Most of the consultants, particularly the young ones, have issues with nervousness. These issues can get worse when they are about to try to sell to a prospective client whose wealth is an order of magnitude larger than that of the clients they are accustomed to dealing with. It's natural. The consultant cares about what he's doing. He understands that if he can't succeed in this type of sales call, he may not be employed by Merrill Lynch much longer. He wouldn't be human if he weren't nervous. But the nervous consultant can sabotage his presentation by overthinking it, by evaluating his performance as it's happening, and thus coming across as stilted and artificial.

Merrill Lynch offers a lot of resources to its consultants in this sort of situation. They're trained in model sales presentations. They can ask a senior consultant, or their boss, to team up with them. They have everything they need to prepare thoroughly. They can and should use visualization, rehearsing the presentation in their minds, imagining all the ways the prospective client might react, all the questions he might ask, and all the ways they'd respond. My role is to persuade them that once this thorough preparation is over, they can put any fears aside and perform instinctively.

The same is true of people just getting started in their careers who get nervous before a job interview. It's unfortunately true that a lot of nervous applicants do poorly in job interviews. They're qualified for these jobs. But they let fear get in their way. They were afraid of the way the interviewer would perceive them. They were afraid that their own nervousness would hamstring their ability to converse intelligently, which is an example of a self-fulfilling prophecy.

I would counsel a young job seeker that process will be his best friend. A big part is the preparation process. It's important to study the company and its situation very thoroughly. An applicant needs to know as much as possible about what the company does, how it does it, its challenges and opportunities. Then he needs to anticipate and visualize all the questions an interviewer might throw at him. Most job interviewers rely on variations on the same stuff, and you need to be ready when the interviewer asks, "What was the most significant challenge you overcame in your last job, and how did you do it?" The applicant can think of his performance process as a means of making certain that all of the positive things he wants to say about himself get placed in front of the interviewer. He listens to the questions, waiting to hear a word or a phrase that he's already decided will serve as a cue for him to raise one of these positive points.

A good process excludes worries about the outcome of the process. I work with the Cincinnati Reds. Like all baseball teams, the Reds want to drive home runners in scoring position. The problem for many big-league teams is that when runners are in scoring position, particularly in close games, the batters' performances are not as good as in situations with no runners on base or in games that aren't any longer close. This shows the detrimental effect of deviating from the hitting process and worrying about the outcome. The irony is that this problem stems, in part, from the fact that the Reds, like a lot of teams, have good kids on their roster, kids who care about the team's success and want very much to help. When this kind of kid gets up in the ninth inning with runners on second and third and two outs, down one run, he's tempted to think about the outcome of his at-bat. "If I get a hit here, the team will probably win. If I don't get a hit, the team will lose." In this frame of mind, the player tries very hard—too hard. Experienced pitchers in this situation will throw a lot of breaking balls that miss the strike zone—knowing that hitters who are trying very hard and thinking about outcomes will be prone to chase such pitches, swinging and missing or making weak contact that results in an out.

I counsel the Reds to make sure that each hitter develops, understands, and follows a performance process. A batter's performance process can't be very complex. Just like a golfer, he needs to have a stance that he replicates before each pitch. After that, hitting is a matter of reaction. Sometimes players simplify it to "See ball, hit ball," and that's not far from the truth. An average major-league fastball takes a little more than four-tenths of a second to reach home plate. A hitter has perhaps a tenth of a second to decide whether to swing. Great hitters can see and process a lot of information in that tenth of a second. They get a look at the ball's initial trajectory. They may see something about the pitcher's hand as he releases the ball. (When the hitter sees the side of the hand, it probably indicates a breaking ball. The pitcher's palm indicates a fastball.) They may pick up something about the ball's spin. But that information processing has to be done at the subconscious level. There just isn't time for conscious thought. If a hitter is relaxed and confident, his subconscious brain can do its best in this process. If he's worried about the outcome of his at-bat, his conscious brain is engaged and the process just doesn't work as well. He won't be entirely focused on the little cues he has to process before deciding whether to swing. The batter needs to get lost in just seeing the ball and trusting that the only thing he can control is letting himself unconsciously react to what his eyes are seeing. Doing so won't, of course, guarantee a hit. But it can make certain that a .300 hitter remains a .300 hitter in clutch situations.

Phil Jackson, the great NBA coach, had another way of expressing the same principle. Jackson said he learned from his own coach with the New York Knicks, Red Holzman, that every shot needed to have the same level of importance. Holzman believed that part of his job as coach was ensuring that the players never got too high or too low emotionally. He didn't want the team overjoyed after victories or distraught after losses. Jackson calls it the middle path. It's the path that enables a performer to keep process foremost in his mind under all circumstances.

This approach can make an individual look placid or even

detached. That doesn't comport with the way our culture expects people to look in these situations. We want our athletes to jump up and down and yell when they are getting ready to play a big game. We want them to exult when they succeed and to sag in sadness when they lose. I try to disabuse athletes of this notion. When a performer is process oriented (unless, of course, we're talking about a singer or dancer) he tends to be quiet. He may have a small smile on his face, particularly when he makes a mistake. He's like still water, lost in the process, minimizing the moment, underreacting to everything.

It's not easy to get to this state. I often tell people that the hardest thing they can try to do is to be themselves when they're doing something they really care about. It takes discipline. I want the basketball player to approach his game as if he were playing golf in the off-season. I want the golfer to think the way he does when he's shooting hoops with some buddies in the driveway.

A lot of golfers can't quite get themselves into that state, because in the back of their minds they hear a voice saying, "You're not trying hard enough. You're being sloppy." But the smart ones eventually get it.

I keep asking players, "When was the last time you hit it out of bounds in a tournament because you weren't trying hard enough?" The answer is, "Well, never."

At the 2011 British Open, Darren Clarke, at the age of forty-three, won the major championship he'd been yearning for all his life by adopting that approach. He made his goals having fun and staying unconscious. He was nervous, of course. But he was devoted to his process all four days of the tournament—he just saw targets and hit his ball to them. That's the way winners overcome nerves.

As I told Darren, "You're unstoppable if you're unflappable."

10.

Evaluating Yourself

'VE LEARNED a lot about the minds of champions by watching the way John Calipari evaluates, pumps up, and criticizes his basketball players at the University of Kentucky. He often does things exactly in the opposite way from what most people would expect—and do to themselves.

Early in the 2011–12 season—the year Kentucky won its first national championship under John's leadership—I was invited to go to Lexington to see the Wildcats play St. John's, a perennially good team from the Big East. It happens that Rob McNamara, the head pro at Farmington Country Club in Charlottesville and a good friend, is a Kentucky native and a big fan of the basketball team. So I took Rob with me. We sat behind the Kentucky bench, and it was a party from start to finish. Kentucky dominated, getting ahead at one stage by thirty-five points. The final score had Kentucky up by twenty-five. The big crowd in Rupp Arena loved it and showed their love from the opening tip to the final buzzer.

Rob and I went down to the Kentucky locker room. Cal

was away in a separate room doing a postgame radio interview. The players were celebrating. And why not? They were young and they'd just thrashed a big-name team.

Cal came into the team room, saw the celebration, and got angry. He told them to quiet down, and then he laid into them. I looked at the players' faces. They were shocked. So was Rob. He looked at me as if to ask, "What's going on?" I put a finger to my lips. We listened.

"Guys, how can you be in here celebrating?" Cal said. "I have been talking to you every day in practice about playing hard. Banging the boards. Diving on loose balls. I've been telling you we have to do those things for forty minutes every night. That is our goal."

His voice grew even sterner. "I have not mentioned winning or losing once all year. I would rather lose the game and have you guys play hard at both ends for forty minutes than win and have you guys start celebrating with eight minutes to go. For thirty-two minutes, you guys played fantastic basketball. You did everything we've been practicing. And then you just totally lost focus. Guys, we're not going to become the team we can become if we don't do it for forty minutes every night. Thirty-two minutes isn't good enough at Kentucky. If it's good enough for you right now, you're going to have to change, because it's not good enough for me. I want you to understand this loud and clear. You better get it."

Cal turned and walked out of the locker room.

"If I ever did that with my pro shop staff, they'd kill me," Rob whispered.

"Well, this isn't your pro shop staff. This is Kentucky. They're trying to be the best of the best," I said.

People who are trying to be the best get used to tough evaluations. They get used to high standards. Sometimes the evaluations come from coaches like Cal. More often they come from within. But it's important that the evaluations come at the right time and are directed at the right stuff.

As I told Cal later, I thought he picked a perfect time to chew his team out and emphasize a key lesson. There's no better time to teach than right after winning a game. That's when people are receptive. That's when they can handle criticism. After a loss, good athletes are already down. They can turn inward and not even hear what a coach is saying.

In this case, the Kentucky team heard Cal's message. He cared more about the process of playing basketball the right way, with sustained effort and unselfish play. He didn't care so much about an early-season win or loss. As I've said, Cal has certain behaviors he wants from his players. They have to run all out. They have to play tenacious defense. They have to rebound and they have to dive after loose balls. They have to do it for forty minutes. He knew that these things would ultimately be more important in determining the success of the season than whether the team beat St. John's in December. They are essential at Kentucky. A player embraces them, or he doesn't play.

Nothing I've recounted about this game so far is likely to be too surprising to anyone steeped in the American culture of leadership. Whether the leader is a coach or a drill sergeant,

we have lots of examples of tough leaders yelling at their charges. And there's a place for that.

But there's another, equally important side to leadership. I suggested to Cal that later that night, after the players had something to eat, he needed to start building them back up. He needed to explain to them why he chewed them out in the locker room. He needed to make sure they understood that he wasn't upset because they won; he was upset because they hadn't met all the standards he set for them, standards they would have to meet if they were to win championships. He needed to talk individually with his players and point out the things they had done well.

Cal didn't need me to tell him that. He already understood it. Part of his brilliance as a coach is that he knows how to evaluate his players. He knows how to criticize them, and he knows how to praise them. During the NCAA tournament later that season, I noticed that Cal and his assistants rarely criticized a player during a game, almost never if the player was hustling. Instead, when Kentucky made mistakes, Cal and the coaches applauded. They weren't applauding mistakes, of course. They were applauding effort. During games, in fact, I have never seen Cal berate a player for missing shots. During games, he seems only to care whether his guys are going all out. In his system, a player can raise his hand and take himself out of the game if he's tired. If he does that, he can pretty much tell Cal when he's ready to go back in. If Cal takes a player out of the game because he doesn't think that player is going all out, it might be a while before the kid gets back in the game, and then it will be Cal's decision, not the player's.

When I talked to the Kentucky team during that run to the national championship, I tried to reinforce the ideas that Cal instilled through his evaluation system. When it came time to play, I didn't want any criticism or any judgment infecting the players' minds. I just wanted them to play fearlessly and joyfully.

They did.

Of course, if you're reading this book, you probably don't have a coach as good as Cal is at deciding when you need criticism and when you need encouragement. You've probably already figured out that in most areas of your life, you're going to have to provide those things for yourself. Exceptional people, in my experience, are almost always good at the tricky art of self-evaluation. Most people are not.

When I work with financial consultants I sometimes ask them to think about how their lives would change if, like professional athletes, they lived in a world where their performances were televised. Imagine coming home at night and having your spouse say, "How was your day?" You'd give the usual reply: "Fine." Maybe you'd add, "Tough day."

And your spouse would say, "Fine? Tough? I don't think so!"

Your spouse might point out that you got to the office early, at seven o'clock. But then you read three newspapers, primarily the sports pages. Then you got coffee and a doughnut in the break room, and you chatted with Stu from accounting about last night's games. Then you sat at your computer, stared at it for a while, and checked your e-mail and Facebook. Then you picked up the phone, as if you were going to call prospective clients, but you must have gotten the phone yips, because you didn't make any calls. Instead, you went back to the break room and commiserated with colleagues about how tough the economy is these days and how the company isn't supportive enough. Then maybe you read some research, and then you went out to lunch with friends. After lunch you checked out some websites. And maybe in midafternoon you made a few calls just to make sure you didn't feel you'd wasted the day.

But tough? Fine? Your spouse wouldn't think so. He or she was watching you, remember? He or she would say you might as well have called in sick and gotten some chores done around the house.

"But," you'd think, "I got to work at seven a.m.!"

This is a problem that psychological researchers call perceived exertion. Average people tend to overestimate how hard they are working. When John Calipari gets new freshman basketball players at Kentucky, he sometimes hooks them up to heart monitors as they practice. When they get to a break, he asks them how hard they've been playing.

Typically, the freshman will say, "Very hard, coach!" Sometimes the freshman will tell Cal he's afraid his heart might burst, he's working so hard.

Then Cal hooks the freshman's heart monitor up to a computer, which produces a chart showing how hard he's working. He shows it to the freshman, and then he pulls up a similar chart from an NBA player during practice. The charts don't lie. They show that the Kentucky freshman is working at about 50 percent of capacity. The NBA player is working at 80 to 90 percent. The difference is one of the differences between playing amateur basketball and playing at the highest level.

I know that organizations and individuals often have evaluations built into the structure of their lives. It begins with the first report card a child brings home from kindergarten and goes from there. I remember doing some work for Pizza Hut and being impressed by how often they inspected and evaluated their operations. They evaluated whether the salad bar items were wilting before they were consumed. They evaluated cleanliness and how often patrons spilled things in an effort to develop a maintenance schedule that would keep each restaurant spotless. Competition forces intelligently managed organizations to evaluate themselves all the time.

But I also know that the evaluations in our lives often don't tell us what we need to know. A report card grade doesn't necessarily reflect the effort a student did or didn't put into the work. When I taught at the University of Virginia, the administration made us fill out and submit evaluation reports each year. But everyone knew how to check the right boxes and fill in the appropriate numbers. The reports ultimately said almost nothing about the quality of the research and the teaching the faculty was doing.

I have found that champions rarely let themselves be influenced much by outside evaluations. They set their own standards, and their standards have much more to do with the process than the outcome. They know that any single outcome can be influenced by others and by luck. Faithfully following a rigorous process sets a much higher standard.

John Calipari's evaluation of his Kentucky team after it

defeated St. John's in 2011 is a case in point. Cal knew that his players were more talented than the St. John's players. The fans might have been happy because of the outcome—the final score. He wasn't. He was more interested in the process—whether his team did the things he wanted it to do for the full game.

There is no end of examples. A financial consultant would be expected to have a rigorous process for evaluating investments he recommends to clients. If he hears a tip on CNBC, recommends it, and his client makes money, he shouldn't evaluate himself highly for doing so. Similarly, a student might cut an economics class all semester and use his fraternity's file of old exams to prepare for the final. He might get lucky and have a professor who recycles old questions and get an A for the final and an A for the course. That A shouldn't delude him into believing he's a good student.

Exceptional people don't delude themselves this way. They compare their performance to the process standards they've set for themselves. The outcome is of secondary importance, because they know that if they honor the preparation and performance processes they've determined will work for them, the outcome will take care of itself. They're process oriented not because they don't care about outcomes, but because they know this attitude leads to the best outcomes.

I worked some years ago with a top-flight amateur golfer named Bill Shean. He decided that when he played competitive golf, he would keep score not by how many strokes he took but by how well he followed his preshot process, mentally and physically, before every shot. His "final score," under this system, would be a percentage rather than the number of strokes he took or holes he won. His goal was to score 100 percent—being faithful to his process before every shot. This kind of self-evaluation worked very well for Bill. He became one of the few golfers in history to hold simultaneously British and United States national championships—in his case, the senior amateur titles.

Bill, like most exceptional people, decided to define excellence in his own terms. The world, for example, might compare home builders by the size of their companies, or their companies' stock price, or some other financial metric. Exceptional people might or might not care about those things. I know a builder who works on one house at a time. He takes great care and great pride in doing a superb job with each house, creating a space that his customers will enjoy living in for decades. He sets his schedule so he has plenty of time for bicycling, his other passion. He makes a good living, but only the people who know him and his work well know how exceptional he is.

Exceptional people know when to evaluate themselves. I don't recommend to golfers that they evaluate themselves in the middle of a round, for instance. I don't have a problem with a player who knows he was mentally sloppy when he three-putted a hole and gives himself a little kick in the pants as he walks to the next tee, as long as that kick in the pants serves to clear his mind and get him into his routine before he drives the ball. But in general, it doesn't pay for a golfer or any sort of performer to evaluate himself in the middle of a performance. Evaluation is a function of the conscious brain, and it's not a good idea to turn on the conscious brain during the performance of a skill best left to subconscious control. A golfer who tends to evaluate himself during a round tends also to start having thoughts like, "I must not be setting the club properly at the top of my backswing," which leads to trying to fix swing mechanics on the course, which leads to making a bad situation worse. If a golfer in midround starts keeping track of the percentage of fairways he's hit, he can start thinking of the last lesson he had on driving the ball, rather than seeing his target and letting the swing happen.

There's a time to think about things like fairways hit, but it's after the round. A smart player might take his scorecard after he finishes. He might tabulate how often he missed a green and got the ball up and down to save par. He might evaluate whether his putting or his wedge play was to blame on the holes where he didn't save par. And that would help him establish his practice priorities for the next week or month.

Exceptional people in my experience are almost always very good at monitoring and evaluating their adherence to a good process and catching themselves when they slip slightly—when they're just half an inch away from where they should be. Average people let themselves get a lot further off track before they catch themselves. The exceptional person, for instance, might make a commitment to a diet and exercise plan designed to maintain an ideal weight. If he falls short of honoring that commitment during the holidays, he will notice when he's gained three pounds, correct his eating, hit the gym hard, and quickly get back to his ideal weight. The average person might fall off the wagon during the holidays and need six months to catch himself. By then he's gained fifteen pounds, and the process of returning to a healthy weight is much harder for him.

Exceptional people often keep separate lists of practice goals and performance process goals, either on paper or mentally. Practice goals might be things like practicing with scoring clubs (the putter, wedges, and short irons) for at least an hour a day. They might include swimming a certain number of yards per day and a certain number of days per week and completing the requisite swims in a certain time. Performance process goals involve things like staying in the present moment, accepting whatever happens as it happens, underreacting to everything, being unflappable, and totally trusting in your skills during competition.

The exceptional person monitors himself in relation to these goals (though not, of course, in the heat of competition) and uses that evaluation for making course corrections.

The question of how good someone can be is only answered after the individual has put in a long period of sustained, committed adherence to a process of improvement. By "a long period," I don't mean days or weeks or even months. Typically, a long period might mean years.

I set no limits on how long a person should work at the process before making a final evaluation of himself. That can be a tough issue for a professional golfer to handle. I've worked with dozens of golfers who have won major championships, but professional golf is a harsh game and I've worked with a greater number of players who never make the field at a major, let alone win one. Each year hundreds of amateur golfers turn pro with dreams of winning majors and making a lot of money. The reality is that most of them don't. Most of them don't even make it to the PGA Tour, where only the top 125 players earn full playing privileges for the next season. They scuffle for a while on minor-league tours where the purses are small and the entry fees are high.

If someone in that category asks me whether he should keep going, I don't have an answer. I have questions. The most basic is, "Are you sure you've honored your commitment?" By that, I mean to ask whether the client has done what he set out to do, which is to make the strongest possible effort to become as good as he can be by creating and fulfilling performance and preparation processes. Has he been living it? Or has the effort been halfhearted? Has he played with belief in himself, or has he failed to build the confidence that would enable him to find his potential?

If the answer to either of those questions is no, then I think it's premature for an individual to evaluate himself and give up. If and when someone decides to quit, he will never know if everything would have fallen into place with one more day or week of sustained effort. The time may come when it's appropriate to give up one dream and start chasing another, but in my experience it doesn't come as early as most people think.

Even when I believe that the time has come, I still don't offer advice. The decision has to be the player's. But at least he will know he's arrived at an appropriate point for self-evaluation.

11.

Going Through the Fire

'VE PICKED up a lot of wisdom from coaches in my career, and one of the best bits came from an old football coach who hailed from what was once the steel mill area of western Pennsylvania. He always said you have to be willing to go through the fire. He was alluding to what happens when you take a piece of metal ore from the ground. In that state, it's loaded with impurities. You put it in a fire. In the fire, its impurities are burned away, and the metal becomes stronger and harder. The fire adds value.

The coach was not, of course, speaking literally about metal. He was speaking about failure. Everyone I've ever met has failed at least a few times. What separates exceptional people from the crowd is the way they respond to failure.

Sport is a great laboratory for testing the way an individual or a team responds to failure. Most of us live lives in which failure can be hard to discern. Unless you happen to get fired or suffer a divorce, your daily activities seldom give you a clear win or a clear loss. But in sport, every day or every week brings clarity. Either you won or you failed. And quite often, you fail.

In golf, temporary failure is a given. No one to my knowledge has ever shot a perfect round of golf. But I will stipulate for the sake of discussion that a perfect round might be 18 under par, a birdie on every hole, for a total of 52, 53, or 54 strokes. If you take a look at the leaderboard of any PGA Tour event, you'll see that no one shoots 52, 53, or 54. No one even comes close. If you just get into the sixties for four consecutive rounds, you stand a very good chance of winning the tournament in any given week. It's a given that any player on the PGA Tour is capable of making a birdie on any hole he plays. That means that on most of the holes, most of the players do not play to their capabilities. They fail.

Tournament wins are rare for even the best players. In the greatest seasons of their careers, Arnold Palmer, Jack Nicklaus, and Tiger Woods won eight, seven, and nine times, respectively. That means that even at their peaks, the very best players in the world won less than half the tournaments they entered. The good players on the Tour are satisfied if they win two or three times a year, or perhaps 10 percent. And for the journeymen, just making it to the weekend feels satisfying. There are a lot of weeks when journeymen miss the cut, win no money, and leave town Friday afternoon, the taste of failure fresh in their mouths. It's similar with many of the athletes I counsel. The best hitters in baseball fail two-thirds of the time, and their teams fail almost half the time.

No matter the sport, an exceptional person needs to learn

to be resilient in the face of failure and adversity. I remember a meeting with Sam Snead at a *Golf Digest* school. Sam was one of the great teachers *Golf Digest* assembled for that school. My role required giving a talk about the mental challenges of golf. I spoke about how easy it is to have a good attitude when you're playing very well. You remember all your great shots. People compliment you. Your head is filled with beautiful images. But when you're not playing well, your memories are of missed putts and bad shots. People ask you what's wrong with your game. It's easy to become discouraged and frustrated.

Sam was no stranger to that. In his autobiography, he talked about how he developed putting problems midway through his career. He was on an exhibition tour in South Africa with Bobby Locke and he missed a few key putts on the unfamiliar putting surfaces down there. Locke, as usual, putted brilliantly. Sam could not shake the memory of those missed putts, and years later, he blamed those memories for the yips that came into his putting stroke.

But when he was young and playing well, Sam said, it was a different story. In those days, as I've said, he'd lie in bed and replay his round in his mind as if he were watching it on television. But when he came to a shot he'd mishit, he would revise the tape he was playing in his mind. He'd erase the bad shot and envision himself making a good one. He'd fall asleep thinking only of good shots, and he would wake up the next morning feeling refreshed and confident.

That's one way exceptional people deal with failure. They refuse to remember it. I've spoken about how Jack Nicklaus believed that he never three-putted on the final green of a major. Sam Snead had a way of editing his experience to erase his poor shots.

I have little patience for the commentators on radio and television who periodically disparage the team that loses in the NBA finals for attending the winning team's victory party. According to these self-styled experts, the losers should have gone back to their hotel rooms and brooded over their loss. That sort of thinking is probably part of the reason those people are sitting in a television studio commentating instead of playing in the finals themselves. The worst thing an athlete can do after a loss is brood about it.

I'm not saying that an individual shouldn't spend any time reflecting on failure. It's obviously important to learn from mistakes. But there's a difference between learning from failure and wallowing in it. On the golf course, it's best to treat failure as an accident. Golfers mishit shots all the time; even the best players on the Tour are going to leave a sand shot in a bunker once in a while. When that happens, almost the worst thing they can do is dwell on it. The shot is in the past, and their minds need to be in the present. The absolute worst thing they can do is not only to dwell on it but also to make harsh judgments about themselves, like "I'm a horrible bunker player."

Instead, when that ball comes rolling back toward their feet after hitting the lip of the bunker, they need to step away for a second, start thinking about the next shot, and trust that they'll hit it really well. Maybe after the round, they can go back and think about why they mishit the shot and determine whether they need extra practice in bunkers or whether they were just trying for a shot that had too little margin for error.

I remember hearing Michael Jordan speak some years ago about a lesson he'd learned from Dean Smith about dealing with failure. Michael had left the University of North Carolina and played a couple of years in the NBA. But he returned to Chapel Hill in the off-season to play pickup games with other Tar Heel alumni and talk with Coach Smith.

On this occasion, he was talking to the coach about how hard it was for him to accept the seemingly cavalier attitude of his Bulls teammates toward losing. After a loss, he said, he would stay in the shower for an hour, replaying everything he did wrong as the hot water pounded over his body. Or he'd sit by his locker with a towel over his head, marinating his brain in images of mistakes. His teammates, on the other hand, would shower and get out of there. Michael thought they didn't care.

Dean Smith disabused him of that notion. He told Michael that if he wanted to become the player he could be, he ought to give himself no more than ten or twenty minutes to reflect on a bad performance. That would be enough to learn everything that could be learned from it. After that, he advised Michael, he ought to think about playing great basketball in the next game—or do something else and not think about basketball at all. "If all you do is keep reliving your mistakes, you're going to destroy yourself," Dean said.

There's a notion in our culture that great performers flagellate themselves with their mistakes. We often hear about team meetings in the National Football League on the Monday after a loss in which the coach plays the entire game film over and over again in slow motion, pointing out everyone's mistakes. I suppose there's some sort of imagined macho code in which the tough guy isn't afraid to confront his errors. But if there are coaches who do that more than once in a great while, I doubt that they are winning coaches.

Yes, good performers learn from their mistakes. But if they are athletes I counsel them to spend, as Dean Smith advised, no more than ten to twenty minutes rehashing what happened in a loss. As they do that, I advise them to pay particular attention to evaluating the way they adhered or didn't adhere to their process during the performance. And I want them to be careful about the way they talk to themselves about it.

For a golfer, to take a common example, it's fine to reflect on a bad shot on the seventy-second hole and think, "I didn't follow my routine on that shot. I let my mind get out of the present. I started thinking about how much a win would mean to me and my family. But just getting to the seventy-second hole with a chance to win shows I have what it takes. The next time I get in that position, I'm going to stay with my routine until the last putt drops. I think the outcome will be different then."

Too often, a player can think, "I choked like a dog. I didn't have any guts. How will I ever win?"

There's a huge difference between the two. Exceptional people are resilient. Resilient people react to failure by finding something they can cling to, some hope for the future.

It doesn't matter if the people who confront failure are

athletes. In any endeavor, things can go wrong. A sales call can turn into a bad, unproductive meeting. It's fine to ask afterward, "What was our mistake? Did we do everything we should have done? Did we do our homework and were we ready to answer this prospect's questions and meet his needs? If we didn't, how can we be better prepared the next time?"

But if your honest analysis after a bad meeting is, "We prepared properly and performed well, and it just didn't go right," then there's nothing to regret. You just have to be determined to get 'em the next time.

The only time to rehash a performance, of course, is after the performance is over. Nearly every athletic contest or performance is comprised of numerous small successes and small failures. A baseball player gets up to bat four or five times in an average game, and he can handle twice that many chances in the field. An actor can have hundreds of lines and a singer may do a dozen songs in a set. A pianist may strike a thousand notes during a recital. No one gets a hit every time. Everyone makes errors. No one hits all the notes exactly right. It does no good to castigate yourself in the middle of a performance. In fact, it hurts. If you miss a note in a piano recital and you start beating yourself up about it, you're more likely to miss subsequent notes because you're not focused properly.

Curiously, most people recognize the right response to failure when they see others display it. Everyone admires the point guard who picks up his teammates after their mistakes. He makes a great pass to give a teammate an open layup. The teammate misses the layup. The good point guard doesn't scowl or pout. He gives the guy who missed the layup a high five as they get back on defense; his body language promises there will be other open looks, other layups, and different outcomes. He makes sure that the breakdown on the offensive end of the court doesn't lead to a breakdown on the defensive end.

People see that sort of behavior and admire it. But they find it hard to apply it to themselves. They want to beat themselves up. What would they think of a point guard who chewed out the player who missed a layup as they ran back to the defensive end, humiliating him and distracting him? Yet they do the equivalent to themselves, silently.

Perfectionists are an extreme example of this destructive tendency. It's hard to argue with the perfectionist's intentions. He has high standards. He works hard. He wants to do everything well—so well that it's perfect. And, of course, he falls short. There's a fine line between trying diligently and being a perfectionist. But it's important to understand the difference between diligence and perfectionism and to stay on the diligent side of the line.

For the perfectionist, nothing is ever good enough and every performance is a failure. You see perfectionists come to grief fairly often at a competitive school like the University of Virginia. High school academics or sports were easy enough that this type of student arrives at UVA still intent on being perfect. It doesn't happen at the collegiate level. On the playing field, the competition is too tough. In the classroom, a few people manage straight As, but no one is flawless. When I was teaching and coaching and encountered a perfectionist, I tried to persuade him to focus on the process rather than the outcome and to be satisfied if he put an excellent effort into the process. It didn't always work. I saw perfectionists become depressed because they felt they always failed. I saw them give up sports they were good at rather than endure their self-inflicted castigation.

Perfectionists almost never arrive at the highest levels of sport. They can't survive. At the highest levels, especially in the pro ranks, so much depends on *not* being a perfectionist, on understanding that there will be losses and mistakes and on responding well to those setbacks.

Years ago, Rick Carlisle, now the coach of the Dallas Mavericks, was a guard for the University of Virginia. Toward the end of the 1983–84 season, he came to me with his tail between his legs. He said, "What's wrong with me?"

I knew what was troubling him. In three close, late-season games, Rick had taken the final shot for the Cavaliers. Each time, the ball spun around the basket and popped out. He told me that kids in his dorm were saying that Jeff Lamp, a great guard who had played for Virginia a few years earlier, had always made the game winner. "I miss them all," he said.

First, I had to correct the record. "Jeff Lamp didn't always make the game winner," I said. (Jeff was good; he later played for the Lakers and other NBA teams and he now works for the NBA. But he wasn't perfect. No one is.) "After you graduate," I told Rick, "all they remember is the ones you make."

This is true. Everyone remembers that Babe Ruth hit 714 home runs; they remember, or believe they remember, that he called his shot in the 1932 World Series. They don't remember that the Babe struck out nearly twice as often as he homered. But one of the ways failure can give people problems is through their mistaken perception that no one else fails, or that someone else, like Jeff Lamp's legend, never failed. People like Rick, who want so badly to succeed, compare themselves to someone or something that never existed.

I congratulated Rick for having the nerve to take the final shot in a close game; not everyone wants the ball in that situation. I told him to stop judging the outcome and confine himself to judging the process. As long as he had taken the shot confidently, believing he could make it, he was doing the right thing, and he ought to keep doing it. He had to keep believing in himself.

Virginia squeaked into the NCAA tournament that year, and then it went on an improbable run. Rick took and made the critical final shot against Iona. Then he took and made the critical final shot against Arkansas. I remember Rick coming into the locker room after that game and giving me a hug. "You were right, Doc," he said.

I laughed. "No, Rick. You were right to keep taking your shot."

Rick went on to play several years in the NBA for the Boston Celtics, then became a coach. His Dallas Mavericks won the NBA championship in 2011. I looked up his record recently, and he's lost 366 times as an NBA coach. So in that sense, he's failed hundreds of times. But he's never been a failure. He's always ultimately won, and over his career has proven himself a real champion.

He knows—and I hope I helped him learn—that how an individual responds to the things that happen to him is more important than the actual happenings. An exceptional individual expects that at least occasionally, he'll lose, whether it's a basketball game, a golf tournament, or a business account. He takes pride not in never having setbacks but in how he responds to setbacks.

Yes, exceptional people sometimes suffer rejection. They apply for jobs and don't get them. They try out for teams and don't make them. They learn from the situation. They refuse to take it too personally, to see it as a sweeping and definitive judgment of their capabilities. If an exceptional person doesn't get a job interview, he thinks, "They don't really know me; they've just seen my résumé. So they didn't reject me. But a time will come when they will get to know me, and when they do they'll want to work with me."

The reality is that if your dream is to accomplish something awesome, it's not going to be easy. If it were easy, everyone would be doing it. People who go for greatness are going to get knocked down a lot. They'll have difficult times. They'll struggle with doubt and uncertainty. People around them will question the wisdom of their quest. The issue is not whether you'll fail, because you will. It's whether you'll get back up and keep going. It's whether you can sustain your self-confidence and your belief in yourself and keep bouncing back.

Failure is only final when you stop striving.

12.

Working Hard, Working Smart

GROWING UP in Rutland, it took me a while to learn the difference between working hard and working smart. Most of the adults I encountered when I was a boy worked hard. They got up early in the morning and worked all day. While they were working, they tried to do their work as well as they could. Sometimes they had two jobs. On weekends or days off, they usually worked around the house. There, as on their jobs, they were meticulous and diligent. I learned a lot from observing them, and the lessons I learned about how to work hard were invaluable to me.

I didn't notice a difference between working hard and working smart until I started to caddie at the Rutland Country Club. On Wednesday afternoons, in those days, a lot of the doctors, lawyers, and other professionals in town would come out to golf. I saw immediately that most of them drove new Buicks, Lincolns, and Cadillacs instead of the older Fords and Chevys that the people in my neighborhood drove. I noticed, of course, that they had the freedom to play golf on a weekday afternoon when the men who worked in the marble quarry and the scale factory had to be on the job.

I listened to their conversations as I carried their clubs, and I noticed that while they were all intelligent men, they weren't obviously more intelligent than my father, or my uncles, or most of the fathers and uncles of my friends. I wasn't quite sure what set them apart, although even then I understood that higher education had a lot to do with it.

Then, when I was in graduate school, I met Nick Tomasetti. Graduate school meant long hours for me. I made some money by coaching lacrosse. I taught in an elementary school for three hours each morning. I taught swimming and tennis all summer. I think for all my work, I might have been making $2,000 to help pay for my education. Sometimes it was hard just to get people to give me what they'd verbally agreed to pay.

Nick was in the aircraft business. He'd worked for Pratt & Whitney, which was a major manufacturer of aircraft engines and other aviation equipment. My enlightenment began when Nick took off on a business trip to France and came home less than a week later with a check for $24,000. I could only look at it enviously. He told me that he'd made it as a commission selling repaired engines that Pratt & Whitney needed to market. During his trip abroad, Nick had earned maybe one hundred times what I'd made working hard on teaching and lessons.

I didn't draw the conclusion that I ought to change careers and get into the used-engine business. But I did start to understand a little better the lesson I'd begun learning on the fairways and greens of Rutland Country Club. Exceptional people did not just work hard. Like Nick, they worked smart.

One of the glories of the United States is the way anyone who wants to work hard can rise to, or stay in, the middle class. Today, it may be a little harder than it was a generation ago; I know that times are tough in many parts of the country. Today a person who is determined to make it into the middle class may have to work more than one job. But it can be done, and it is being done by millions every day.

Exceptional people are rarely satisfied with being in the middle.

They may not define success in a monetary way, which is fine with me. Someone exceptional may decide that he wants to grow organic vegetables and live on a self-sustaining farm. He'll be determined to grow the best organic vegetables in the world, and I'll admire him if he manages to do it. An exceptional person may dedicate himself to working with the poor or working for a church, knowing that by doing so, he limits his income. That's also admirable in my book. But many exceptional people want their earnings to be commensurate with their abilities and success, and that's also fine with me.

If you want to make more than a middle-class wage, it's not enough to work hard. Working hard is the minimal standard for exceptional people. It guarantees that you can live with yourself. It doesn't mean you'll win, but it means you'll be able to handle losing. Vince Lombardi often said he could live with a loss, or even a losing season, if he knew that he and his team had sustained their commitment to hard work during the off-season and in practice the week before the game.

But to make it into the upper middle class or the upper class, or into the ranks of championship teams and players, you have to become a strategist about your work. You have to have a bigger vision. You have to have a better belief. You have to have some really good ideas that you can use to leverage your hard work. You have to have something that makes you unique.

If you look at the wealthiest people in the world, they tended to get that way by having other people work for them. They didn't do all that work themselves. Many of them have learned to make money while they're sleeping or on vacation.

Let's suppose, for instance, that you're an accountant and you have a desire to be exceptional. For the first seven or eight years of your career, you have to understand that you will need to work long hours. You're learning. You're picking up experience in what clients expect and need. You'll doubtless be judged, in part, by the number of hours you work. And you'd better not let too many people outwork you. Typically, you'll get promoted just because you're perceived as a hard worker and the extra hours will pay off. But after that, you may have to distinguish yourself in other ways. You may have to figure out methods for adding value to what you can do for clients, advising them on their strategies as well as keeping their books. You may have to start your own practice and employ others.

Early in an exceptional person's working life, he may work

for little or nothing, just because he's passionate about what he does. When I was starting out, I coached Charlottesville kids in tennis for free, on my own time. I didn't consider it a burden. I did it because I liked working with athletes. I had the sense that I was honing my coaching and counseling abilities. But I really didn't consider it work. The first few professional golfers I worked with got my services for free. Again, I got a kick out of working with them, and I didn't mind the hours I put in. I was learning. I know that in many professions, the hours are long and the pay is low at the start. Doctors, in their residencies, put in eighty-hour weeks for nothing like the income they'll generate when they're older. Graduate students teach classes for a minimal stipend as they work on their advanced degrees. That's just the way it is.

But after a while, that changes. If you want to move into the upper income brackets in most fields, you've probably got to become more entrepreneurial. If you're in the food business, for instance, you can probably become a restaurant manager by working long and hard hours for several years. But if you want to take the next step up, you'll need to go from managing a restaurant to owning a restaurant and then to owning a string of restaurants. To succeed at that, you'll probably need a shrewd understanding of the dining market and the concepts that will intrigue and satisfy today's customers. Maybe they want less fat, salt, and sugar in their food. Maybe they want a place that hits the sweet spot between the drive-through and white-tablecloth service. Maybe they want a place that evokes a night out in Marrakech or Mexico City.

You'll need to learn about topics ranging from finance to zoning. Instead of being a good employee, you'll need to figure out how to identify, hire, and keep good employees.

Golfers have to go through a similar process, and not all of them can make the transition. In their junior years, kids can easily separate themselves from the competition by outworking everyone. These are the years when a golfer lays down the basic neural pathways of the game, teaching his subconscious brain how to direct a proper swing. Repetition is at its most valuable.

But there comes a time when merely staying on the range longer than anyone else doesn't work so well. I've seen a lot of golf tournaments, but I've yet to see one that hands out a check for hitting the most practice shots.

The perception persists that sheer hard work remains the sole key to success in golf, but it's a myth. Maybe Ben Hogan was the golfer most responsible for this idea. Hogan indeed worked very hard when he was young, teaching himself a swing. And he was famous for dourly advising golfers that "the secret is in the dirt."

Actually, when I spent a day with Hogan back in 1989, he was anything but dour. He was chatty, talkative, friendly, and personable. He was just full of stories. I asked him about his practice habits, and he told me something I hadn't expected to hear. It wasn't about the dirt or how many hours he worked. It was about a golf fixture from a bygone era called the shag boy. Back when Hogan was young, there were no buggies with a driver's cage trundling around the practice range picking up practice balls. In fact, practice ranges were rare. Golfers who wanted to practice would go to an unused corner of the course. They had to bring their old golf balls with them in what was called a shag bag. If they didn't have a shag boy, they had to pick the balls up themselves after they'd hit them.

Even when he was struggling financially, Hogan told me, he tried always to practice with a shag boy. The shag boy gave him a target and made his practices more realistic. Hogan told the shag boy that he'd like him to catch every ball on the first or second hop, and he didn't want the boy to run after any of them. Hogan's shag bag contained no more than eighteen to twenty-one balls. He'd start with his lofted irons and work through the shag bag with each club. As his skills increased, he got to the stage where he would routinely hit the ball within a couple of steps of the shag boy ten times in a row, a dozen times in a row, maybe fourteen times in a row. At that point, he would start to replicate the pressures of playing tournament golf. He wanted to run through the bag without missing the shag boy, just as he wanted to hit fairways and greens in a tournament. He was tempted to start trying to guide the ball to the shag boy, just as he was tempted to start trying to guide or steer the ball in a tournament. He knew that he played his best golf when he *didn't* try to steer the ball, when he just looked at his target and trusted that his swing would get it there. So it's a myth that Hogan made himself great merely by working hard, by beating balls out of the dirt till his hands bled. He did it by working smart; working smart made him into a better tournament player, the kind of player who could and did close the deal in the last round of a major championship.

"There was no transition for me from practice to tournament play," Hogan said.

My longtime friend Bob Christina is a teacher of golf, an assistant coach at the University of North Carolina–Greensboro, and a professor emeritus of kinesiology. He's had a long career studying how people learn motor skills like the golf swing. Bob and his colleagues have figured out that athletes can accelerate their learning by moving beyond simply beating balls on the range. Bob's got a raft of proven ideas about training aids and drills that, used properly, can speed the process. He espouses a principle called "desirable difficulty," which states that a player will develop skills faster if he introduces the right sorts of complexities and challenges to his practice time. To take one example, it will help if he uses his short-game practice time to chip and pitch from a wide variety of lies. One of the basic ideas is that a player has to understand how to make his practice skills transfer to the golf course and to competition.

Ben Hogan figured out something like these principles on his own, and they accelerated his development. He practiced a lot, yes. But when he practiced, he told me, he'd never just beat balls. He'd hit those eighteen to twenty-one balls from his shag bag and he'd take a break—smoke a cigarette or drink something. During the break, he'd think about what he was doing, the ball flight he was seeing, and the ball flight he wanted. Then, refreshed and purposeful, he'd go back to work. He worked hard. But he separated himself from the other golfers of his generation by working smart.

Good players today are figuring out the same things. I see

smart players going out onto my home course in the twilight with a shag bag. They find one of the toughest driving holes on the course, well after any players have come through. As it gets dark, they tee up three to five balls and practice driving them on this difficult hole. They get much more out of their practice time than they would if they spent that time driving balls into the wide expanse of the practice range. I see good players tamp down a patch of sand in a practice bunker with their feet, then practice hitting chips and pitches off the packed sand lie. It's another way of maximizing the efficiency of their practice time, because it helps them deal with the tightest of lies. These are the players who, when they need to, can pitch the ball off the putting surface to get around an obstacle like the little doughnut-hole bunker in the middle of the sixth green at Riviera in Los Angeles. Golf course designers are more and more frequently surrounding greens with tightly mowed chipping areas. These players don't get flustered when their ball winds up in one. They can see the target and hit the ball without worrying about the lie. I used to teach with Davis Love Jr., father of the present Tour player and former Ryder Cup captain Davis Love III. He taught players to practice iron shots out of fairway bunkers. He thought the difficulty of hitting the ball precisely out of the sand sharpened the benefit of practice. He was right. I see good players apply this principle during practice rounds by shifting their balls onto sand-filled divot scars rather than taking the easier shot off the fairway grass. Good practice is usually harder than the competition it prepares you for.

On the other hand, I work with amateur clients who are

determined to master golf by working very hard at it. They love practicing. They hit ball after ball after ball, trying, for example, to ingrain a deft, accurate short pitch shot from a tight lie. I wind up working to get them to understand that in some phases of learning golf, less can be more. I counsel them to emulate Hogan by hitting a relatively small number of balls before taking a break. I tell them to use their full routine before every practice shot they hit, envisioning the shot they want, taking a practice swing, taking their grip and stance in a very precise way, then letting the swing happen without thinking of their swing mechanics with their conscious brains. I tell them that the quality of their practice shots is more important than the quantity. It's a tough lesson for some folks to learn. They look with yearning eyes at those little pyramids of practice balls that high-end clubs and courses feature on their ranges. They've grown accustomed to patting themselves on the back for every pyramid they reduce to nothing. Those pyramids, I think, are like the all-you-can-eat buffets at some restaurants. They can be dangerous.

Life isn't always fair about how much work is required to succeed. Some golfers win with less practice than others, because the game comes a little easier to them. Jack Nicklaus won eighteen major championships not in spite of spending a lot of quality time with his wife and kids, but in part because he spent a lot of time with them. He understood that for him, refreshing himself by immersing himself in his family was probably better for his game than standing on the range beating balls day after day. Of course, he made himself the best player in the world before he made that decision.

Like Nicklaus and Hogan, great coaches have realized the importance of efficiency in multiplying the fruits of hard work. John Wooden practiced his great UCLA teams only ninety minutes a day. But every moment of that practice was programmed by Wooden and his assistants not only to teach the players but to condition them. Wooden's teams almost never wilted in the fourth quarter, in part because they practiced very hard for those ninety minutes—almost always running—but in part because they practiced *only* ninety minutes. When that time was done, Wooden and his assistants might continue to work, planning for the next practice or game. But he wanted the players to go back to their dorms, study, and leave basketball at the gym. His teams stayed fresh all the way through March.

John Calipari also limits the duration of his practice sessions, but he makes certain that the players work hard during every minute. In the final half hour, he tells them that the final thirty minutes are the time when they'll separate themselves from their competition by driving themselves against fatigue.

Those principles apply to just about everyone who wants to be exceptional. Work very hard at reaching your goals, especially when you're young. But as you get older, keep in mind that to continue to rise, you have to work smarter, more efficiently, more strategically. And when it's time to go home, leave your work at the office.

13.

When to Heed the Competition and When to Ignore It

I N SPORT, I find that exceptional people tend to have the same attitude toward the competition. They pay attention to it during their preparation, but they try to ignore it during their performance.

I want my golfers, for example, to ignore the competition when they're on the course. That seems paradoxical to many people. A golf tournament seems at first to be inherently about competition with other people. If you shoot ten under par for a tournament, you won't win if someone else shoots eleven under par. I get that. Nevertheless, I want players to feel as if they're in their own little world as they walk around the golf course—in a bubble, if you will.

I want them to feel that way because exceptional golfers, including exceptional competitors, understand that the primary competition is themselves. They understand that the biggest struggle is always the one within, the struggle to bring their best physical and mental self to the first tee and maintain that presence until the last putt falls. It's a formidable challenge. They understand that the primary opponent is the golf course, not the other players in the field. If they can meet the challenge of the golf course, if they can master themselves, they know they can be happy when they look at the leaderboard at the end of the day.

I don't, for these reasons, advocate looking at leaderboards and reacting to the standings during play. I want the golfers I counsel to have a game plan for the course they're playing, a game plan that is designed to give them the best chance to shoot the lowest score they're capable of. If their game plan is sound and the object is to shoot the lowest possible score, why would they want to change it just because they see, say, that Rory McIlroy has birdied three consecutive holes to move to seven under par? What happens when players start reacting to the competition is usually bad. Instead of thinking only about the shot at hand and where it fits in their game plans, they start thinking about the future, about who's going to hold the trophy in an hour. They might start to aim at sucker pins, thinking they absolutely have to have birdie—and make bogey instead when their ball finds a bunker.

A lot of golf fans and golf commentators want to argue with this. They always ask, "But suppose you had a course where the final hole was a long par five, and you were a stroke behind after seventy-one holes. Wouldn't you want to know that when you decided whether to try to go for the green in two?"

Not really. I want a player to have a game plan that says that if he drives the ball into the fairway within a certain yardage of the green on that eighteenth hole, his best chance to make birdie is to go for it. If he doesn't drive onto the fairway within that yardage, his best chance to make birdie is to lay up and rely on his wedge and putter. The game plan is designed to give the player the best possible chance to make birdie under all possible circumstances. Why would he want to change it because of what someone else had done?

Gary Koch, whom I've worked with in the past, was broadcasting a tournament recently and said that if a player didn't want to look at leaderboards coming down the stretch in a tournament, he ought to find another profession. That's a fairly common sentiment from high over the eighteenth green in a tower. Down on the ground, I understand that there may be players who benefit from looking at a leaderboard, who can use the information to focus ever more sharply on the shot they must play next and the routine that will help them hit it to the best of their ability. But they are outnumbered by the players who won't benefit, who will let the information from the leaderboard distract them from what they must do.

Great coaches have understood this. Bill Walsh of the San Francisco 49ers wrote a book toward the end of his life called *The Score Takes Care of Itself.* The title summarizes his philosophy. He believed great teams turned in great performances not by looking at and reacting to the scoreboard but by preparing meticulously and executing their game plans as close to perfectly as they could. He wanted his players to focus on their preparation and performance processes, not on the score.

I understand that it's not always possible to avoid looking at leaderboards. Modern tournament courses have so many of them, displayed in such prominent locations, that a player sometimes can't avoid seeing them. Whether the look at the standings is purposeful or accidental, I think it's imperative that after taking that look, the player gets his mind back into the present moment and, essentially, forgets about the standings, focusing tightly on the shot at hand.

The best players understand this. I saw Lydia Ko give an interview recently after she won the Swinging Skirts LPGA Classic in a tight race with Stacy Lewis, who was then ranked number one in the world. A nongolfer might have expected that Lydia, who was only seventeen at the time, would decide that Stacy was the player to beat and focus on doing that. Not so. "I told myself I was going to go out there and play some good golf and not pay any attention to the other players or Stacy and what they were shooting," she said. "If someone plays better than me, then so be it. I can't control what they shoot. But I can control my game and my concentration."

I'm not surprised that Lydia recently became the youngest golf pro ever to rank first in the world, a feat she achieved while still a couple of months shy of her eighteenth birthday. She understands the mental game in a way that takes some players many years to learn.

The great coaches had similar philosophies about competition. They didn't pay it much mind during games. Vince Lombardi didn't care that everyone knew the Packers were going to run their sweep many times in each game. It didn't matter to him that opposing coaches were telling their players to be alert for Jerry Kramer and Fuzzy Thurston pulling out to block. He just wanted the Packers to execute the play properly, the way the team had trained and drilled to do it. He had confidence that if they did that, the play would work. John Wooden, in much the same spirit, didn't do much in-season scouting of the opposition during UCLA's glory years. He wanted the Bruins to run their offense and their full-court press the way he'd coached them to do it. That was a lesson he learned from his own coach at Purdue, a Midwest legend named Ward "Piggy" Lambert. Lambert taught Wooden not to worry about the opponents. If the team played its own game, the opposition would be forced to adjust and follow. If Lombardi and Wooden did much scouting it was during the off-season, when they might give some thought to preparing for the challenges they would face. But their emphasis was always on making their systems and their playbooks suit their personnel, not adjusting to what the opposition did.

Of course, a very important part of that approach is contained in the words "played its own game." A Lombardi team or a Wooden team that played its own game was playing on a very high level indeed. Ignoring the competition isn't going to work if it means being complacent or being mediocre. But in sport, assuming you have very high standards, doing what you believe in is more important than anything the competition can do. In sport, playing your own game is what exceptional people and teams do when they compete. A good pitcher whose mainstay is a slider that breaks low and away to a right-handed hitter is going to use that pitch regardless of whether the scouting report says teams will be looking for it or that a certain player does well against low, outside pitches. He's going to use his best pitch.

The preparation process for competition differs from the performance process in that you must be mindful of the standard the competition is setting, at least in a general way. When I was playing college basketball, I was one of the few players who lifted weights as part of my preparation. Now weight training is considered essential, part of the minimal effort a player who wants to compete in college has to put in. He must be aware of the fact that his competitors are lifting weights. If he doesn't get stronger, he won't play. Women who want to play in the LPGA these days have to heed the competition from Asia. They've got to put in more practice time than Babe Didrikson Zaharias or Mickey Wright ever did. If they're kids with aspirations to play professionally, they can't be satisfied with the practice standards of their hometowns, where a girl who hits balls for an hour every day is considered a hard worker. They have to be mindful that girls their age in Asia are practicing four or five hours a day.

That's the nature of sport. The bar moves higher. Jack Nicklaus had the record of Bob Jones's thirteen major titles to compete against. Tiger Woods competes against Jack's record of eighteen majors. If a young golfer today wants to try to be the one to break Nicklaus's record, he needs to be aware of the competition. He needs to know the level he'll have to attain if he wants to beat the world's best in nineteen major championships. He needs to know, in general, how well they hit the ball, pitch it, and putt it. He will need to prepare accordingly.

I have one caveat to add about when to heed competition in your preparation process. It's important not to compare yourself to the precocious. Yes, Tiger Woods was winning golf tournaments at the age of six or so. And you, more than likely, weren't. More than likely, you hadn't even started to play golf at that age. And there are other famously talented people who don't seem to work very hard to attain excellence, although I suspect that more often than not in those cases, the individual prefers not to practice in public. (The majority of men and women on the pro golf tours had to work their tails off to get there, and they work their tails off to stay there.) You can't decide that because you weren't winning golf tournaments at an early age, you don't have the innate talent to compete with people who were. And you can't decide that since Player X seems to get by with very little practice, you can, too. You've got to compare yourself to people who are similar to you in ability and development. You've got to compare your work ethic to theirs. You've got to figure out what you need to do to excel, then do it, regardless of what others are doing.

But comparison in preparation is important. I've seen the influence of competition on the preparation process recently in college basketball recruiting. Recruiting is an essential part of the preparation process if you're a college coach who wants to win. Many coaches, if they're being candid, don't like recruiting. They've got things they'd rather be doing than attending AAU summer-league basketball games so they can stroke the egos of sixteen-year-old boys. This is why some coaches and their programs ascend to the elite ranks and then plateau and decline. The coach in his early years works very hard to get players who can help him win. After he achieves success, though, the coach decides he can leave the dreariest recruiting work to his assistants. He lets them hit the road, sleep in motels, and attend AAU and high school games. He takes on the role of the closer, meeting with recruits when they make their campus visits, sealing the deal that his assistants have prepared. But then he finds that that approach doesn't work as well as doing it himself.

John Calipari has raised the bar in college basketball recruiting. Cal has a way of getting the best high school basketball players to play for him. He always competes within the rules. He gets the players he gets because his credibility is very high. He doesn't make promises he can't keep about playing time. He tells players and their parents that he will only promise to work them very hard and then offer his honest advice when the time comes for them to choose whether to stay in school or turn pro. This approach works for Cal because kids know Cal's track record. His players do well in school as long as they choose to remain there. They stay out of trouble. They develop their talents in a unique showcase that the NBA respects as an incubator of talent. They get drafted and they succeed.

Cal has never shirked the scouting and home visits and hand-holding that go with recruiting. I think he relishes it. As a result of the success he's had, I have started to see other coaches intensifying their efforts. Some of them are elder statesmen in the coaching ranks, men who had reached the point of handing off a lot of the recruiting chores to their assistants. Now they're back in high school gyms and at summer camps, because they realize that if they want to compete with John Calipari, they have to start by working at least as hard as he does. That's the nature of sport. In the preparation process, you have to be very aware of the competition, and the bar only moves one way—up.

The line between performance and preparation isn't so clear in many other endeavors, and people whose business isn't sport have to adapt their attitude toward the competition accordingly. In some areas, the competition is only marginally relevant. Seal, for instance, doesn't and shouldn't worry about Justin Timberlake or all the other singers out there trying to sell recordings and concert tickets. If he did, he'd probably only make his own performances worse. He just needs to make sure he's putting everything he has into the songs he writes and sings.

But there are other businesses where the competition can wipe you out quickly if you aren't aware of it and don't adapt to it. Twenty years ago, I remember reading an article about mobile phones that asked, "Will anyone ever catch Nokia?" That was before Apple, Samsung, and other competitors got into the business in a big way. Nowadays, it seems that it would be hard to find a kid without a smartphone, but Nokia has lost so much of the market that Microsoft gobbled it up in 2013. The decay of a business's competitive position can set in quickly, as it can with teams and individuals.

Generally, I am a firm believer in the value of competition. When I consult with businesspeople and they tell me how tough their competition is, I sometimes ask them to compare themselves to players on the PGA Tour. On the Tour, only 125 players are fully exempt, meaning that they can enter the standard Tour events (though not invitational events like the Masters) whenever they want to. Not many marketing managers, lawyers, or accountants would thrive in an environment where only the top 125 producers in the world could keep their jobs. Moreover, on the PGA Tour, the list of exempt players is compiled anew every year. No one can have a couple of good years, then coast for a few years. On top of that, at nearly every tournament there's a cut. Only the best seventy players in that week play all four rounds and get paid. If your business were as tough as the PGA Tour, and you weren't one of the top seventy performers in the world on Monday and Tuesday, you'd still have to pay for your office space, your phone, and your computer that week, but you wouldn't get paid and you'd have to wait until the next week to try again.

That would be pressure. Most people understand that this pressure works very well for professional golfers. (In fact, there are old pros like Jack Nicklaus who will tell you that the quality of golf would be higher if no one got paid unless he won, rather than just made the cut.) But the same people who see the value of competition on the PGA Tour don't want their jobs to be that competitive. Most of us would like to do our own thing and be safe and secure for life.

I understand that safety and security are nice to have. But safety and security can become more important to an individual than being exceptional and doing fantastic things over the course of a life. When that happens often enough in a society, the society begins to die. It gives up its leadership role in the world. Accepting the importance and necessity of competition keeps us alive inside. It forces us to be honest about ourselves.

This may not be a source of comfort to someone who's

worked hard in a business that is being squeezed by new competition. I know reporters who used to work for newspapers and magazines in jobs that no longer exist because of competition from the Internet. I am sure that there are chemists and engineers who worked conscientiously making film for Kodak, and I know it's not their fault that digital photography has pretty much replaced film. I have a cousin who runs a building supply company in Rutland and has done an excellent job of it for decades. It's not his fault that Lowe's and Home Depot moved into the area and started selling supplies at prices he simply couldn't match.

My cousin reacted by working harder and smarter. He decided that if he couldn't match the prices of the big chains, he would compete by offering customer service the chains wouldn't match. He offers design services for kitchens and baths. He offers convenience. In Rutland these days, if you want to start a project at six a.m. on Sunday morning, you can buy your supplies from my cousin and be confident that they'll be delivered exactly where you want them, at six a.m. He offers superior quality, trying to appeal to high-end contractors who just can't risk getting some warped two-by-fours in a load of wood. But it's tough to compete. He's had to lay off staff, which is painful to him. He works long hours, which is painful to his family.

In this, he's similar to the Cincinnati Reds, the major-league baseball team I consult for these days. The Reds are in a competitive situation that seems unfair to some eyes. They are a small-market team that must play and try to beat big-market teams, like the Chicago Cubs and the Los Angeles Dodgers.

Those teams have massive broadcasting deals and they can afford payrolls the Reds will never be able to match. The Reds do not waste any energy bemoaning this situation. They compete. They understand that they have to do a better job than the Dodgers or the Cubs in scouting and drafting talent. They have to be better at developing that talent in the minor leagues, so they have to hire better coaches. They have to do a better job preparing the minds of the players in the organization, which is why they have me. When I speak to the coaches and staff, one of the things we all stress is doing a better job of accepting and welcoming the reality of the Reds' competitive situation. "Can you love the challenge of this reality?" I ask them. And I tell them that if they can be successful with the Reds, they'll have proven their worth as baseball men.

Really, they have no alternative. Nor does my cousin in Rutland. Lamenting the fact of tough competition in the marketplace would be like complaining about the weather. It's there. It has always been there. The marketplace would not function without it. And, like the weather, it brings many benefits. Yes, competition may have become more intense in recent years as the globalization of the economy has subjected American companies to new, disruptive forces. But the economy has been subject to competition since long before Henry Ford cast a cloud over the business model of buggy makers.

Economic competition can give you a chance to develop the quality of psychological hardiness. When I was beginning my psychology studies, stress was thought of as a great danger, as a cause of depression and psychosis, as something to be avoided. People used to say, "Don't get stressed out," almost as often as they now say, "Have a nice day." But that was when the notion of learned helplessness was also very popular, when psychologists tended to think that most people had a limited capacity to handle stress.

We've since learned to the contrary that stress can help people grow, just as stressing a muscle by lifting weights helps it get stronger. I think exceptional people have always intuitively understood this. They've understood that they need tough competition to become the best players they can be.

I remember a meeting some years ago that Tom Kite arranged for me with some of his friends on the PGA Tour. This was after I'd started working with Tom but before many professional golfers had ever heard the term "sports psychologist" or knew anything about the subject. Tom talked, and then I talked about what Tom and I worked on. The players listened. Then one of them asked Tom, "If this stuff works, why are you having him tell us about it?"

Tom replied, truthfully, that he felt there was more than enough money on the PGA Tour to give him and a lot of other pros a handsome living. He was not about money, even though he would win several yearly earnings titles. He wanted to see how good he could get at golf, and he understood that he needed the competition of his peers to push him to the highest level he could reach. So he was willing to share information he thought would make everyone a better competitor. That's how a psychologically hardy person embraces competition.

I understand that in the business world, there may not be enough money to give all the players a good living, and competition can tend to be more like a zero-sum game. If you own a local bookstore, and your customers start deciding that it's more convenient to buy from Amazon.com, you're probably going to need some creative ideas just to stay afloat. You're going to need some brilliant ideas to grow and prosper. Maybe your future won't be in book retailing at all.

But no good will ever come of whining about competition. If you're going to be exceptional, you must embrace it.

14.

When to Be Patient and When to Be Impatient

'VE SPOKEN already about some of the lessons I learned from a golfer and teacher I came to revere, the late Paul Runyan. He started playing as a touring pro back in the early 1930s, when the PGA Tour was little more than a handful of club pros driving three or four to a car from one southern city to another during the winter months. (During the summer, they had "real" jobs, making equipment and giving lessons at clubs in the North.) He was a walking library of information about both the golf swing and the history of the game.

I met Paul when we both worked as instructors at schools organized by *Golf Digest*. This was maybe half a century after Paul's debut as a touring pro. I gave a talk in which I mentioned teaching young players to believe they could win on the tour from the first tournament they played. When it came time for questions, Paul raised his hand.

"That was a very interesting talk, Dr. Rotella," he said. "But when I was coming up I was taught to respect the veteran players and to learn our trade from them, to get experience. I was taught that I really shouldn't think about winning for five years or so. It sounds to me like you're not teaching that and it seems like it might be viewed as disrespectful."

"Great point," I said. "How many times did you win in your first few years?"

"I didn't," Paul said.

"That's why we don't teach that kind of patience anymore," I said.

Paul was a lifelong learner, and although he was by then in his seventies, he asked me out to dinner so we could talk some more about when to be patient and when to be impatient, and when to be respectful of others and when to be respectful of yourself. The notion that a young professional golfer might not feel entitled to win immediately seems strange to our ears, living as we do in a time when Kentucky wins national basketball titles by relying on freshmen and Tiger Woods and Rory McIlroy started winning majors in their early twenties. But the idea of waiting your turn wasn't as odd to Paul's generation. Paul and his peers entered the game when professional golf was more like a guild, with well-understood distinctions between masters and journeymen, and journeymen and apprentices. (The PGA, in fact, still calls beginning pros "apprentices.") In those days, young pros knew, or were taught, their place. They didn't eat in the members' dining room at the clubs where they competed. They deferred to their elders. They couldn't be on the Ryder Cup team, no matter how well they played, until they had served an apprenticeship on the Tour. Byron Nelson wrote that when he was a touring player, he would often give exhibitions at clubs, playing a round with some local luminaries. He said he always made it a point to find out who held the course record and what it was. If the record was held by the host pro, Byron made sure not to break it. Paul was from that school.

At dinner, I explained to Paul that I certainly didn't want the young players of the moment to disrespect what veteran golfers did in the past. But I did teach rookies to believe they could win as soon as they teed it up. I taught them to understand and respect the achievements of their elders but to keep in mind that the elders hadn't beaten them, the rookies, when they won their titles. Why, I would ask my clients, would you believe someone can beat you until he proves it to you? I was teaching, in effect, impatience. I was teaching that if they wanted to play on the Tour, they needed to believe they were ready to win and deserved to win.

I knew that no one on the modern PGA Tour formally considered himself an apprentice. But in their minds, some young players gravitated to a lower rung of the Tour's informal pecking order and felt comfortable there, at least for a few years. They set modest goals, like making cuts and winning just enough money to keep their playing privileges. They did not see themselves as ready to win. They thought they needed experience. There is value to experience, but there is also value in the innocence that comes with lack of experience. And as William James ("People tend to become what they think of themselves") could have predicted, the clients who wanted to wait until they were more experienced to think they could win didn't win. If I challenged my clients on this, they would often say they were just being patient. And patience, as we all know, is a virtue.

Except when it isn't.

In fact, part of being exceptional is knowing when to be patient and when not to be. There are indeed times when part of being exceptional is being patient. I have a client who has been phenomenally successful in the business world, rising from modest beginnings to become a corporate chief executive and make a lot of money. He took up golf when he was about forty, and he's joined some of the best clubs in the country. He's in great physical condition and he hits the ball a long way for someone now pushing sixty. He reasons that since he can drive the ball as long as the good amateurs he plays with and is a better natural athlete than they are, he has the potential to play on their level. And he does have that potential. He quickly figured out that if he were going to realize that potential, he needed to learn to chip and pitch and putt the ball really well. So he took short-game lessons from an excellent teacher, and he practiced those shots. When he came to talk to me, he was frustrated. His short game still wasn't good enough for the competition he wanted to play in. He responded to this as he might have responded to lagging results from a company he'd purchased and wanted to turn around.

"When is it going to get really good?" he demanded.

In his case, I had to counsel patience. I told him that he had to keep working with the teacher he'd chosen, because his understanding of the fundamentals was good. We went out to the short-game practice area at Glenmore, where I live, and we worked on his short-game routine, on visualizing the shots he wanted and trusting his technique. After a while he got better, and he was excited about that. But the next morning, he was struggling again for the first forty minutes or so. Then, again, his results got better.

That was the nature of golf, I told him.

"You're going to go backward sometimes and you're going to get lost sometimes," I said. "When that happens, you're either going to stick with the techniques and fundamentals you've learned or you're going to ask someone for a 'tip.' If you ask someone for a tip, he'll give it to you. And then you'll be trying something new, and it might be different from what you were originally taught, and you'll wind up more lost than ever."

Instead, I said, he had to be determined to stay the course. "Stick with it until you get it, but don't think it's going to be a straight shot. Be patient. It will come. I don't know how long that will take. I just know it will. When the day comes that your short game is where you want it to be, you'll be so proud of the shots you'll be making. It will be a joy. But until then, you just have to be patient and keep working at it."

I felt hopeful that this client would understand and accept what I was telling him precisely because he was such an exceptional individual in his business life. In this case, the exceptional person is the one who can accept the vagaries of the improvement process, keep working at it, and be patient. Most people don't have this kind of patience. They get too frustrated to stick with an improvement program if they don't get immediate results. They might give up and accept the idea that their short game will always frustrate them. They might give up golf entirely, thinking that it's too hard or they just don't have the talent to play well.

Improving at golf takes patience. So does competing at the highest levels.

On the PGA Tour, the golfers I counsel need an extra helping of patience. Tour players don't often come to me because they've been winning too much. They seek my help because they don't feel they've been winning enough. They feel that the results they've been getting are not commensurate with the talents they have or the work they've been putting into the game. When they think this way, impatience can sabotage their chances.

On the Tour, or in any high-level competition, an impatient golfer thinks he has to force the issue. He knows that in an average event, the winner is going to finish between ten and twenty strokes under par. Consequently, if he starts the tournament with an even par round, he gets impatient. He feels he has to try to make birdies happen instead of letting them happen.

What's the difference between trying to make birdies (or any results) happen and letting them happen? It can be subtle. It can be a matter of firing at a "sucker pin," a flag perched on the edge of a green that's guarded by water—and seeing the ball go into the hazard. A patient golfer understands that the Tour, or the committee that selects the hole locations, is going to choose a certain number of them that are too dangerous to aim at, depending on the distance of the approach to the green, of course. (If a Tour player has a wedge in his hands, he should be able to aim at virtually any pin; if he can't be that accurate with a wedge, he won't be a Tour player very long. With a long iron or a fairway metal, it's a different story. Patience is required.) In his game plan, the patient player accepts this rule and decides that on holes with sucker pins, he will aim for the center of the green and be happy with a birdie putt from twenty or thirty feet. The impatient player may aim for that sucker pin from two hundred yards out. He may pull out his driver on a tight hole and drive into trouble. He may run a birdie putt ten feet past the hole. He may simply take his mind out of the present moment by thinking about the birdies he didn't make on previous holes or the birdies he thinks he has to make on future holes.

I work with a player on the Champions Tour who got there not by winning a lot of money on the PGA Tour but by coming up through the qualifying school after a career as a club pro. So he's always had to work to maintain his confidence and feel secure. He came to me one winter, wanting to talk about why he'd narrowly missed making enough money to keep his playing privileges for the coming season. In his mind, it came down to the weekend rounds in the final tournament of the year. He had never been a good three-wood player, but in each of those rounds, he'd let his caddie talk him into going for the green with his second shot on a par five—with the three-wood. He made a bogey and a double bogey on those holes. At the end of the year, he calculated that if he'd just parred those holes, he would have finished twenty-seventh on the season-long money list, instead of thirty-second. The top thirty-one retained their playing privileges. His impatience, he realized, was very costly. I think it was born of his insecurity.

When his caddie suggested that he pull his three-wood and go for the green, he had the feeling that an elite professional golfer ought to be able to hit that three-wood, even though the reality is that elite pros often avoid making shots with particular clubs they don't trust. They understand that the object of the game is to shoot the lowest score, not show off their ability to hit every shot with every club. That's one reason they're elite.

Patience is not something one buys, owns, and has forevermore. It can be ephemeral. In recent years, I've seen even Tiger Woods look impatient as he's struggled. I've seen him leave an approach shot under the lip of a green-side bunker. The lie was such that a patient player would choose just to hack the ball out somewhere on the green, take his bogey, and move on. But Tiger tried to finesse a shot close to the hole, presumably because he thought he couldn't afford to take a bogey. He left the first shot in the bunker, blasted out, and, rattled, three-putted. He turned a bogey into a triple bogey by being impatient. He used to be one of the most patient players golf had seen. He played very conservatively on most holes, because he was confident he could make up for the occasional bogey. He waited for others to make mistakes. When he was at his best, I never saw him choose a shot he didn't know he had an excellent chance to pull off. But at times now, he does. When he does, he looks like a lot of players who are worried they aren't going to win and force shots that end up preventing them from winning.

A lot of the players I work with start to learn about patience when they see that the ultimate winning score in an event is not what they thought it would be on Thursday evening. I hear this when they call me on Sunday night. "Doc, if I had known that twelve under was going to win this week I would have been so much more patient out there. But when I teed off Thursday afternoon, I saw that so-and-so had already shot eight under in the first round. So I figured that it would take something like thirty under to win. I took so many ridiculous chances I didn't need to take. I shot a high score Thursday because of that, and then I thought I really had to take chances Friday just to make the cut."

I tell these players that the real opponents are themselves and the golf course—that they should always try to do the best they can with those two foes. If they take what the golf course gives them and win the battle to stay within themselves, they will get the best score they're capable of on that particular day. I point out that Jack Nicklaus won a lot of his eighteen majors by shooting 70 in the final round, not shooting 64. It's true that legends are made by final rounds in the midsixties, like the final 65 that Arnold Palmer shot to win the 1960 U.S. Open. That kind of story occupies an oversize place in the minds of many golfers. In their minds, it seems a player has to shoot a 65 to win a major. But the reality is that many tournaments, especially majors, are not won in legendary fashion. They're won by guys who play a solid two or three under par on Sunday and let the field back up. If you win enough tournaments like that, you'll be a legend.

I work with a young pro who had a lot of success as an amateur. Winning has come more slowly in the professional ranks. At one tournament, we talked for a couple of hours.

When we were done, his mother asked me, "What did you talk about for so long?"

"Patience," I said.

"Two hours about patience?" she asked.

"Well, let's see," I said. "We talked about your son being patient with himself. We talked about him being patient with his swing. We talked about being patient with his scoring clubs and with his short game. We talked about being patient with his putting and not becoming frustrated, trying to force it in the hole, running it ten feet by, and three-putting. We talked about being patient on par fives. We talked about being patient when he's four under and has a two-hour thunderstorm delay. We talked about being patient with playing partners who are ridiculously slow. We talked about being patient with his game when he is hitting it great and putting it great and still has no birdies after eleven holes. We talked about being patient when the wind's blowing. We talked about how, in golf, if you want to be really good, you have to get good at waiting. Most people aren't brought up to be really good at waiting. Little kids tend to be impatient. But at every level he reaches, and the better his skills get, the more patient he will have to be."

His mother looked at me and said, "Goodness! Glad you had that talk!"

She might have said, if she'd been reading along with you, "Wait a minute. Didn't you tell Paul Runyan you taught young players not to be patient, not to wait their turn, to believe they could win?"

Well, yes. But there's no contradiction. Exceptional people

are impatient with limits others place on them, like the notion put forward by veteran players that newcomers need to wait to win. Our last three presidents—Bill Clinton, George W. Bush, and Barack Obama—didn't wait for a consensus among the wise men of American politics that they were ready to lead the country. They saw an opportunity, they believed in themselves, and they seized that opportunity. In that regard, they are exceptional people. An exceptional writer, for instance, would not be patient with someone who told him, "You need to work for newspapers or magazines for ten years before you think about publishing a novel." An exceptional lawyer would be impatient with a senior partner who kept him at semiclerical tasks well after the young lawyer believed he was ready to be a lead litigator.

But exceptional people show enormous patience when they're working at a process they believe will make them better, like the process that leads to winning golf tournaments. Just because the results aren't immediate, they don't give up. They persist. They wait. They don't know when their efforts will bear fruit. They only know they will.

15.

Surrounding Yourself
with the Right People

THE FIRST time I worked with Hal Sutton, he told me a story. When Hal was a young golfer, his father supported his play, financially and in every other way. Hal and his dad heard stories about the pro at Austin Country Club in Texas, Harvey Penick. This was before the publication of *Harvey Penick's Little Red Book*, and Harvey's reputation as a molder of champions was a word-of-mouth thing, passed along from one member of the golf community to another. The best advertising for a golf teacher has always been successful play by his pupils, and Harvey had a lot of successful ones, including Ben Crenshaw and Tom Kite.

Hal's father, who was well-off, put them on a private plane and they flew to Austin for a lesson with Mr. Penick, which Hal remembered might have cost $5 an hour in those days. They arrived at the club and met Mr. Penick. They went to the range. For forty minutes, Hal hit balls, using all his clubs. And all Mr. Penick said was, "Nice shot." Sometimes he varied it a little, saying, "Very nice."

Finally, Hal's father got impatient. "Mr. Penick," he said. "We've got twenty minutes left. You haven't told my kid anything yet. We flew all the way from Louisiana. You've got to tell him something."

Mr. Penick looked at Hal's dad. "All I can tell you, sir, is that I think your son has a really nice action, and I think the best thing you can do is not let anybody touch it."

By the time he told me this story, Hal was a veteran of two decades in pro golf, and his career had gone up and down more often than an elevator.

"If I had just one thing I could change," Hal said, "we would have listened to what Mr. Penick said."

Hal and his dad, of course, hadn't taken Mr. Penick's advice. Over the years, like most tournament golfers, he had had many teachers. All of them had been well meaning. But they all had egos, and they all saw themselves as the man who could refine Hal Sutton's swing and help him realize his potential. Hal was, for a while, known in the media as "the next Nicklaus," because he and Jack were both blond, were both burly, and both hit the ball a long way. Every teacher thought he knew how to change Hal's swing so Hal could live up to that media-imposed expectation.

But if there was one thing about Jack Nicklaus that Hal should have tried to replicate, it was Jack's disinclination to let anyone except Jack Grout tell him anything about the golf swing. Jack Grout had been young Nicklaus's first teacher, at Scioto Country Club in Ohio. After Nicklaus became a successful tournament player, he went to Grout for a few days of refresher lessons on his fundamentals at the start of every season. Grout rarely did what many prominent teachers today do, which is go to tournament sites and work with players on the range. He believed that a golfer ought to know his own swing and his fundamentals well enough to catch himself if he started to mishit the ball and fix the problem on his own. Jack Nicklaus, consequently, was a very self-sufficient golfer.

That, I think, is a big reason why he was able to win consistently for so long, capturing major championships for nearly a quarter century. Jack Nicklaus understood that the fundamentals of success for a golfer encompass more than just the right swing and putting techniques. To be successful, a golfer has to be able to surround himself with the right people, people who will support and encourage him and give him a kick in the pants when he needs it, people who will tell him the things he needs to hear, even when those things aren't always the things he wants to hear. And he has to tune out other people.

It sounds easier to do than it really is. No one, not even Jack Nicklaus, wins as often as he would like. When things aren't going so well, there is always a multitude of teachers' names floating around the putting green and the practice tee at a tournament, almost as if they were being chirped by the birds. It's very tempting for a player to think that he can turn his season or his career around by changing teachers. So, many players make changes, repeatedly. The problem is that while all good teachers believe in certain fundamentals, they all like to tweak the details and they all present those fundamentals in different ways. So a player can subject himself to a barrage of apparently contradictory advice. With different, conflicting ideas flitting through his mind, a player gets worse instead of better. It's easy to get lost.

I, of course, work with players on those same putting greens and practice ranges, and I get many clients by word-of-mouth referrals. But one of the first things I will advise a player is to select a swing teacher (and, these days, an agent, a mental coach, and maybe a nutritionist and a fitness consultant) he trusts and stick with that choice. Sometimes that costs me a little business because I don't fit into that strategy. I don't mind.

You might think that it would be easier for a player to go it alone. That, after all, is part of the Ben Hogan legend, and Hogan was one of the all-time greats. The legend has it that he worked by himself to perfect his swing, putting in countless hours of lonely practice to achieve near-perfection.

As with most legends, there are elements of truth in that narrative. But in fact, Ben Hogan didn't work entirely alone. His wife, Valerie, functioned as a kind of sports psychologist. He tried to quit many times, and she didn't let him. Valerie and Ben, when they were on the Tour, always went to dinner with other players; he had buddies among his fellow competitors. They exchanged ideas about the golf swing. Ben Hogan may not have had formal lessons, but back then there were fewer formal lessons and more informal exchanges of ideas. Most of the great players of that era learned less formally than the players of today. But they didn't learn entirely on their own.

The lesson for people striving to be exceptional is not to try to do it completely alone. You're going to need other people on board with you. You need to select those people carefully, and you need to treat them right.

Those people must believe in you and your talent. I have worked with athletes who were highly successful in college, earning All-American accolades. They were drafted by the pros, but their pro careers never took off the way their college careers had. As I've said, this turns out to be because these athletes lacked innate self-confidence. They fed off the fact that coaches in high school and college believed in them, made them the go-to guys on their college teams. Without that support, they stopped being stars. The belief of others can be very important.

An athlete often can't choose his coach in team sports; that's one of the challenges. I learned this very early in Rutland. I was cut from the JV basketball team at my school when I was in the ninth grade. (The JV was mostly for tenth graders.) I thought I was the best basketball player of my age in the entire town, and I thought I belonged on the JV. This coach was saying I wasn't good enough.

Unbeknownst to me, the coach talked about this to my dad, who was his barber. The coach told my father that not only was I not good enough for the JV that year, but I probably never would be. I'd get a chance to play for the freshman team that year, but freshman ball would most likely be the last time I'd play organized basketball. Fortunately for me, my dad was a wise man, and he chose not to tell me about this coach's opinion until seven years had passed and I had been elected captain of my college basketball team. Because of my dad's wisdom, I was free to think what I naturally wanted to think after he cut me from the JV: "Well, that guy's a poor judge, and I'll show him."

Looking back on it, I am a little more sympathetic to the coach who cut me. I was, after all, less than six feet tall, without exceptional jumping ability. He was making a superficial judgment about me, but it was the same judgment a lot of people would have made. In many ways, he did me a favor. He gave me a lot more motivation, even if it was a negative sort of motivation—the desire to show him how wrong he was about me. He taught me that it was foolish to judge someone else before you could assess that person's mental qualities— qualities like tenacity, diligence, and confidence under pressure. I use that lesson to this day. I never make a judgment about a golfer's potential based on an hour or two of watching him hit balls on the range and putt on the practice green. I need to know about his inner qualities, and those aren't so quickly apparent.

That coach in Rutland also taught me something about the way exceptional people deal with coaches, mentors, and all the other authority figures they encounter in their lives. When they find someone who believes in them and their ability, they latch on to that person. They develop a relationship of loyalty and mutual support. They learn from that person. When they encounter a coach or a boss who doesn't believe they have it, they have the ability to ignore that person. A bad coach or a bad boss affects them only in that they want to prove to the world how foolish he is.

The pro golfers I counsel are generally more fortunate. They're able to choose not only their own coaches but all of the important people who surround them, except for their parents and siblings. I try to impress on them that making the right choices is almost as important as honing their golf skills.

Since a lot of my clients are young men, one of the most common choices they face is the choice of a wife. I've spoken about the special demands on the wife of a touring pro. If a client asks my advice, I tell him to think carefully before he makes a decision. The right kind of spouse can not only add happiness and love to a player's life. She can be a tremendous asset to his golfing career—if she believes in him, supports him, and is always there to encourage him. I've talked already about how difficult the job of a spouse is.

I should be clear here. I do not believe that a spouse is any less entitled to the life of his or her choosing than an athlete, a business executive, or anyone else striving to be exceptional. I do not believe the spouse of an exceptional person is in any way less important. But the reality is that the person striving to be extraordinarily successful will almost certainly have to work long hours. Evenings and weekends may be consumed. Vacation time may be scarce. The spouse of an exceptional person understands, accepts, and deals with this. To outsiders, it may seem that the spouse has accepted a subordinate role. Inside the marriage, I think the partners perceive these to be equal roles.

So when a golfer finds a spouse who wants this life and can succeed in it, I strongly advise cherishing that spouse. This means leaving any golf problems at the course. There are stretches in every professional golfer's career when he's missing cuts and playing, by his standards, poorly. During one of those stretches, when a player comes back to the hotel, I want him or her to nevertheless be a smiling, charming, loving companion. The worst mistake a player can make is to use a spouse as a receptacle for all the doubts and fears he has, to constantly tell her that he's playing lousy golf and doesn't know if he'll ever win. In my experience, a spouse will follow, support, and believe in a player who projects his own self-confidence. She'll do it for a long time. But staying with a complaining, whining spouse who plays tournament golf for a living is like helping someone with a broken leg make the Bataan Death March. Not many people can endure it. If a player needs someone to whom he can vent his doubts, complaints, and fears, that's what sports psychologists are for.

After a spouse, a touring pro needs a coach. The criteria for making the choice have a few things in common with the criteria for picking a spouse. Perhaps even more than knowing the swing, a golfer's coach needs to be supportive. He needs to believe that the player can succeed. He needs to pump up the player's confidence.

This doesn't mean he never criticizes. Of course he does. Otherwise, the player would not improve. Good coaches can sound very harsh with their players in practice, even profane. But being harsh and profane isn't good coaching. When I watch good coaches conduct practice, I indeed watch them get on players, and they can be merciless in pointing out mistakes, especially mental mistakes. But their criticism is always followed by instructional feedback. The template is, "You're doing X, and it won't work. You need to do it this way." More often than not, the coach demonstrates the correct technique. Then practice resumes. Good coaches are aware of how the athletes they work with respond to criticism, and they realize that the response can vary from one individual to the next. They sense which members of the team take criticism too personally and respond as if it were an attack on them, not an effort to fix a flawed technique. The best coaches make sure they always find a way to have all their players enter competition feeling confident about themselves, regardless of what was said in practice.

If a successful coach has a public persona that is one-dimensionally harsh and profane, you can be sure that persona is the product of flawed media portrayals. The media always latched on to the toughest, harshest things Vince Lombardi said to his players, and a superficial observer might have thought that toughness and harshness were all there was to Lombardi's coaching techniques. In fact, he found enough ways to let his players know he believed in them and even loved them that years after his death, they cherished the memory of their time with him; he was still inspiring in their post-football careers.

I still remember what Packer Hall of Famer Jerry Kramer said about Lombardi. He was asked about Lombardi's toughness. He replied, "All I remember is that once when I was really down, he came into the locker room and put his arm around me and told me that before it was all said and done, I was going to be one of the greatest linemen in the history of the game."

Not all coaches understand how to do this. Some years ago, Jim Lefebvre, who was managing the Seattle Mariners, asked me to come out to spring training to observe as his coaches worked with a young outfielder named Ken Griffey Jr. Jim and the rest of the Mariners organization understood what a gifted young player Griffey was. Jim wanted me to watch batting practice incognito. My job was to help him determine whether the coaching staff was working with Griffey in a way that would help him reach his potential. I watched for three days. Apart from Jim, the coaching staff didn't know who I was or what I was doing.

I watched, and then Jim introduced me to his staff. I told them that I loved what the hitting coach was doing with young Griffey. During batting practice, the coach stood by the cage and called a shot to Griffey with each pitch—line drive to left, high fly to right, and so on. Whatever the coach called, Griffey would hit. He and the coach both seemed to be having fun with it, and it was developing Griffey's bat control skills. Griffey was happy that the coach wasn't lecturing him about technique. He looked like the gifted hitter he indeed became, and I congratulated the staff on this approach.

A coach who worked with catchers couldn't stand this. "That's the biggest bull I've ever heard in my life," he said. "The kid's talented, and we're going to pussyfoot around with him and be afraid to change his batting technique when he needs it. That's ridiculous. The kid's got a whole bunch of things that need to be fixed. I can't believe that's what you're telling us."

All I could do was reiterate that I thought the hitting coach had the right approach.

Jim Lefebvre agreed with me. He looked at the protesting coach and asked, "How long were you in the big leagues?"

"Eight years," the coach replied.

"And what did you hit?"

The answer was something in the neighborhood of .210.

"Why would we want to teach him to hit like you?" Jim asked.

The protesting coach actually jumped across the table and started a fistfight with Lefebvre. It quickly devolved to a wrestling match, as baseball fights tend to do. Then it was broken up, and we all actually had a good discussion.

I tried to make the point that developing young talent is one of the toughest jobs in sports, and the first priority has to be making sure that coaching doesn't make the athlete worse. I didn't say this at the meeting, but there are coaches out there who think that developing an athlete means only criticizing him. There's some ego and insecurity attached to this. Not many coaches have the serenity that allowed Harvey Penick to tell Hal Sutton's dad that he had nothing to offer in the way of swing improvements. Sometimes, I am sure, there's a bit of jealousy at play as well, just under the surface. The coach may be jealous of the athlete's superior physical gifts. That jealousy fuels his harsh approach, though the coach probably thinks he's just giving the athlete what the athlete needs.

Some coaches also subscribe to the idea that an athlete can be overconfident. As I've said, I don't, and I won't until

I start hearing players tell me they blew leads in tournaments because they were too confident. But there are people in our culture who worry about the arrogant athlete and fear he'll be spoiled and lazy. So they feel the need to pick the player apart, to demean his abilities. They don't care if they undermine his confidence by doing so.

There may be successful coaches who only bombard their charges with constant criticism, but I don't know any. Think about it. Successful players can't be the sort of people who fall asleep filling their minds with self-criticism, telling themselves they'll never be able to drive the ball straight, make the important six-foot putts, or play well in the clutch. Why would they want a coach who persists in doing that? Yes, a coach needs to work with a player to correct flaws. He needs to give the player honest feedback. Sometimes, that means telling the player that his swing isn't good enough or his work habits aren't good enough. But he has to know how to do it constructively.

Once a player finds a coach with these qualities, I advise treating that coach with almost as much care as the player lavishes on a good spouse. He needs to be loyal to that coach. There are times in a player's development, especially in the teen years, when it may be necessary to seek a new coach who can help the player to higher levels. But that's not often the case for a touring pro. A touring pro who sticks with the same coach gains clarity and stability in his golf game. A player who flits from coach to coach often winds up confused.

Loyalty means more than steadily writing checks. A player who has a good coach ought to cultivate that coach. He ought to show up for lessons, on time, warmed up and enthused. His attitude should be, "I love what you're teaching me. I may not quite do it yet in competition. But I know I'm going to get there." When a coach encounters this kind of attitude, his instinct is to redouble his efforts, to do whatever it takes to help that player succeed.

With everyone in his retinue, a golfer needs to remember to check his attitude. No matter how many tournaments a golfer wins, or how many rings a basketball player amasses, or how much money he earns, he is not bigger or better or more important than anyone else. I've seen athletes spoil their careers because they forgot about this. They started wanting their families to treat them like celebrities, and when the families refused, they got annoyed. Troubled personal lives ensued. I think athletes whose families *don't* treat them as celebrities tend to stay more balanced and more focused.

In most nonathletic careers, as with golf, I don't see many people becoming exceptional on their own. Where a golfer might have to find a swing teacher, people in other fields have to find different kinds of mentors and partners who will help them learn and succeed. For a graduate student, this might be a professor. For a law firm associate, it could be a senior partner. In the financial services firms I work with, young associates are automatically paired with older, more experienced hands. The same principles apply, whether the work venue is a practice green, a lab, a classroom, or an office. Exceptional people reward the people who help them by being loyal, enthusiastic, and helpful.

And just as athletes can wind up with a bad coach, a

coach who doesn't believe in them, people in other fields can experience a bad boss. When they do, they need to respond much as athletes do. They need to find resources within themselves. They need to build confidence on their own, to work even harder, and to vow to prove that boss mistaken. They may need to change jobs to do it. That is, unfortunately, part of life.

Golfers may have a problem that doesn't present itself to people in other fields. In most endeavors, an individual needs to seek out a mentor and considers himself lucky to find a good one. In professional golf, the problem can be too many would-be mentors trying to catch a player's ear and give him advice. If a professional golfer on the range at a Tour event hits a ball that curves too much in one direction or another, then turns around and asks, "What did I do wrong?" there may be half a dozen people within earshot who are quite ready to offer advice. Athletes have to develop a filter that tunes out nearly all of this. Once they have selected a coach whom they trust, they understand that they need to listen only to that coach when it comes to their swing. Otherwise, their minds can be paralyzed by a welter of conflicting ideas and suggestions.

Even with that coach they trust, I've noticed that great athletes have filters. They'll listen to a coach say three or four things about their golf swings. They have a sense of their own abilities, a sense of what they need, and a sense of what will work for them. They pick the one thing that seems most likely to help them, and they latch on to it. They may put the others aside for future reference or they may ignore them completely.

Different people have different learning styles. As a coach and a counselor, I understand that if I deal with two players who have seemingly identical putting problems, one player will latch on to one suggestion and use it, and the other may latch on to a different one and use that one. One player may decide that he needs to envision an actual line on the putting green and try to get the ball rolling on it. Another may need to envision the ball falling into the hole. I don't care, because the suggestions are not contradictory. They're just different ways of getting to the same result. In the same way, if I were asked to teach two children how to figure out half of a given number, I wouldn't care if one heard me suggest dividing by two and the other latched on to multiplying by 0.5. Exceptional athletes don't care, either. They just have a sense of what works for them.

I've noticed that exceptional people also have a sense of the sort of friends who work for them. I don't mean that they employ their friends. I mean that they surround themselves with people who have the same sort of optimistic, confident attitude that exceptional people strive to cultivate within themselves. As Harvey Penick famously advised, they don't go to dinner with bad putters. Attitudes can be contagious. If you're a golfer, you don't want to spend your dinner hour listening to people moan about how nothing's going in, the greens are bumpy, and their luck's worse. They want to hear things that are going to help them make putts the next day.

In the same way, if you're a real estate developer, you want to cultivate friends among people who are excited about the opportunities they have and the projects they're working on.

You don't need to go to lunch with people who are moaning that interest rates are too high and the government won't let them do anything.

I find that successful golfers, and successful people in general, also select their friends based on shared values. In the world of golf, as in any occupation, you're going to find some philanderers. You're going to find some heavy drinkers. And even if the philanderers and the drinkers also have good attitudes about their putting, the players who seek to be truly exceptional won't hang out with them. They sense that eventually, some of your friends' and associates' values and behavior will rub off on you. It's a lot easier to live a successful life if you never force yourself to deal with the consequences of foolish, destructive behavior.

Smart coaches and smart institutions understand this and cultivate an atmosphere in which an individual's good qualities are reinforced and his bad qualities are suppressed or compensated for. This is one reason why John Calipari's basketball players are so often invited to hang out at his house. He wants to create a family atmosphere for his team. He does this because he genuinely likes and cares about his players. But he also knows that at his house, he sets the tone. His attitudes about work and success will be the dominant attitudes. And that helps his teams win.

At the United States Military Academy, the goal is to produce successful soldiers and officers, men and women who will show true grit under the greatest possible stress, the stress of combat. West Point does this in part by creating small support groups for each individual. From the moment the first-year cadets arrive, they're ground down. Some drop out quickly. West Point expects this. West Point even wants this, because it knows that the survivors will start to feel tremendous pride in their resilience, their hardiness. The academy tries to make sure that each individual also feels the same degree of pride in the resiliency of her small unit. Once that group pride takes root, all the good habits the academy wants instilled get reinforced. The bad habits are replaced. No one wants to let his unit down. Everyone in the unit wants to buck up the weakest members. It's an example of peer pressure at its most constructive. The cadets wake up each morning and check on the way each group member is feeling. They fire up the ones who are tired or discouraged. They give their units and themselves nicknames as a way of creating unit cohesion. To the outside world, a cadet might be Joe Smith. But within the unit, he's Badger, and Badger is a tough kid who takes whatever the army can dish out and never quits.

Peer pressure of the opposite sort can sabotage a person's ambition to be exceptional. I counsel a lot of kids who aspire to be collegiate athletes, then become doctors, lawyers, or bankers. They tell me that they intend to play their sport and maintain a high grade point average, so they can get into grad school. I always encourage them to believe they can handle the double load of high-level sport and high-level academics. But if they tell me they also plan to join a fraternity or a sorority, I hesitate. There's nothing inherently wrong with fraternities and sororities. But the reality is that a lot of fraternities and sororities are full of people who value partying, drinking, and drugs. If a kid joins one of those groups, the group will pressure him to put its priorities higher than the kid's original priorities—sport and study. That can't help a kid. It can make the double load of sport and study impossible to carry, and the burden that gets dropped first is usually the academic one.

I've even seen this sort of damaging peer pressure come from within a team. I worked with a golfer from a Big East school who won the conference championship when he was a freshman and didn't progress much after that. When he first talked to me, he unburdened himself of a feeling of heavy guilt. He felt he was sabotaging not only his own golf development but that of the other players on his team.

"Last week was spring break," he said. "Instead of staying at school and practicing, I decided I was going to the Bahamas and partying and not even bringing my clubs. So I convinced everyone on the team except one to come with me. We all went to the Bahamas and got blitzed and went crazy all week. No one touched a club for about nine days, and we have a tournament coming up the day after tomorrow. I'm sabotaging my teammates, and the truth is I'm doing it so I can stay on the team and play even if I don't practice."

That sort of thing happens in a lot of peer groups. The only thing unusual about this kid was that he had the honesty to admit what he was doing. A lot of people operate within their peer groups in an analogous way, but they would never admit it. They're not consciously thinking they want to sabotage others in the group to make themselves look better. But at some level, that's what they're doing. It may be the colleague from work who suggests heading to a bar instead of staying late at the office and working. It may be the fraternity brother or roommate who ropes you into a party when you need to be studying. But the underminer within the peer group is someone that people with ambition, people striving to be exceptional, learn to look out for and avoid.

I wish I could have gotten to know the one kid on that Big East team who refused to go to the Bahamas that week. He sounded like a kid who might be trying to become a champion, and I love working with kids like that. That kid was one among perhaps twelve, and that's about the ratio of exceptional people to average people I find in life. More often than not, people go along with their peer group and settle for the general level of achievement within that group. Exceptional people refuse to do that. They surround themselves with, and listen to, people who will help them be great.

16.

Doing What You Love or Loving What You Do?

THE GREAT John Wooden spent important portions of a long and fruitful life thinking about how to become successful. The result of his thought was the famed "Pyramid of Success," which he taught to generations of UCLA basketball players, summer camp kids, and anyone who was interested enough to ask. John Wooden was a generous man, and he believed that what he had learned about success would help people lead happier, more productive lives. So he shared it freely.

Wooden's pyramid had some of the virtues you might expect a basketball coach to stress, like industriousness, team spirit, and conditioning. But at the very base of the pyramid, acting as one of the foundation blocks, was one that might not be quite so obvious: enthusiasm.

It might seem as if a basketball coach could take for granted that his players would be enthusiastic. After all, they were presumably playing a game they loved. But John Wooden took nothing for granted. He didn't assume, for instance, that his players already knew how to wear their socks and lace up their sneakers. He covered those skills early in every season, just to make sure that nobody got blistered feet. So he didn't assume that just because a kid played basketball for UCLA, he was enthusiastic about it. Wooden preached enthusiasm, and since he was so successful, I would be willing to bet that he instilled it.

Why was that important?

To borrow an analogy from chemistry, enthusiasm acts like a catalyst that makes all the other attributes of a champion's mind work better. Persistence, to take one important example, is so much easier when you're enthused about what you're doing. Sticking with something you love is like biking downhill. Sticking with something you don't love is like biking uphill.

The comedian George Burns appeared on the Disney Channel when he was about ninety years old, talking to a group of kids who looked to be about ten years old. One of the kids asked Burns about the rules to live by that had helped him live so long and well. George Burns didn't have a long list. It's simple, he said. Do what you love or love what you do. I would find it difficult to think of anything better to say to a kid starting out in life.

In the sweep of human history, the ability to choose to spend your life doing what you love is a relatively recent development. For most of our ancestors, there were very few or no choices. A man worked the land or in a factory job. A woman kept the house and raised the children. They might choose to pull up stakes and emigrate. But even in their new homelands, choice was limited.

My paternal grandfather came to the United States from Italy. He worked in a quarry, cutting and moving stone. I have no way of knowing whether he liked the work. Long before I was born, a slab fell on him and killed him. The Depression was raging, and my dad and his siblings had to scrap to survive. There was no question of their picking a career because they loved it.

One of the community members in Rutland helped my family out by taking my dad into his barbershop as a kind of informal apprentice. I'm confident my dad didn't grow up dreaming of being a barber. Having observed him for all of my life, I know his true passion is reading and learning. If he'd been born when I was, I suspect he would have gotten an advanced degree and found a calling that allowed him to keep learning all the time. Maybe he would have been a scholar or a researcher.

Since that path wasn't open to him, my dad took the second of George Burns's two options. He got enthused about barbering. He was president of the barbers' union. He was the first barber in town to learn to do hairpieces. He was the first to learn to do razor cuts. He did whatever he could to separate himself from anyone else in Vermont who was cutting hair. He even found a way to work his passion for reading and education into his barbering. He read widely every night so that whatever the interests of a customer might be, my dad would be able to hold an intelligent conversation while he cut the man's hair.

My siblings and I were the beneficiaries of opportunities that my dad and his father could only dream about. We got the chance to do whatever we wanted with our lives, to do what we loved. Originally, as I've said, I thought my calling was playing basketball. My dad never discouraged me from thinking that, even though he was, I'm sure, cognizant of the fact that I had few of the physical attributes of the average Boston Celtic. He did, however, insist that if I wanted to play sports, I had to get good grades. Thanks to my dad, when my interest in sports morphed from playing to coaching, I had the grades to pursue a higher degree.

I quickly found that my strengths lay not so much with devising plays but with motivating kids. So I gravitated toward psychology and not toward Xs and Os. Figuring out where your real talent lies is an important part of remaining enthusiastic about what you do, and I have been blessed in that way. I still wake up happy every morning because I know that I'm going to get to spend my day doing something that energizes me—working with people who want to be the best at what they do. There is a huge benefit to putting your energy into something you're talented at.

I am hardly alone in this, of course. Thanks to the peace and prosperity enjoyed in the United States and many countries during the years since World War II, millions of people have had the opportunity to decide where their true talents lie and pursue their passions. For many of them, this has led to happier lives.

But every piece of human progress raises new issues and problems. For example, many parts of the world have conquered famine and hunger, only to be faced with a plague of obesity. In the same way, people now have the opportunity to chase their dreams. That opportunity, though, doesn't mean that people always make practical choices. In fact, it allows them to make what seem to outsiders to be impractical ones.

I talk every week to young people who have chosen to pursue tournament golf, because competitive golf quickens their spirits like nothing else in their lives. It's a choice fraught with difficulties, beginning with the fact that for every golfer making a million dollars a year on the PGA Tour, there are a hundred scrapping for a few dollars on minor tours you've never heard of. And yet, tournament golf is an immensely practical pursuit compared to some I see young people choosing today. There have always been kids who want to be movie stars, or rock 'n' roll singers, or painters. Now we also have kids who want to be skateboarders, or equestrians, or artisanal bakers. Compared to skateboarding, tournament golf almost seems like a sure thing.

Periodically, I run into a parent whose grown son or daughter is pursuing this kind of passion. Often, that parent will say something like, "Dr. Rotella, I don't want my son to have to do a job he hates. But couldn't he do something where he'll make a decent living? What if he wants to get married and have kids? How will he support them?" The parent may ask me to try to counsel the child to find a more practical and lucrative way to make a living.

I don't do that. Who am I to tell a kid he's chosen the wrong path? When I started out, the field of sports psychology barely existed. I taught tennis to youngsters for free because

I enjoyed doing it. I counseled athletes because I loved coaching. My father would have been perfectly justified if he had told me I ought to stop coaching for free and find a good, stable high school teaching job where I could coach on the side. Who can know whether a kid's passion for skateboarding won't lead him into posting knockout videos on YouTube, attracting an audience and advertisers, and making a good living at it? No one can.

John Calipari's father told me a story about his son's passion. We were at the NCAA Final Four and Coach Cal was by then obviously successful and well-off. But his dad remembered a different time. The elder Calipari was a steelworker in western Pennsylvania, in the days when steel mill work was a tough but reliable way to support a family. Young John loved both playing and teaching basketball, and one summer, home from college, he worked in several basketball camps as a counselor. He was making $43 a week, which with John's schedule came to well under a dollar an hour. His father talked to some friends and found John a job at one of the steel mills for $14 an hour. John refused to take the job. His dad said, "Why don't you take it? You'll make all the pocket money you need for college next year."

John looked at his father and said, "I want to do basketball. Believe me, Dad, this is what I love. This is what I'm going to be good at."

"I remember thinking, 'This kid's nuts,' " John's father said to me. "But I guess it worked out okay."

That said, if a kid asked me what I thought about a career in surfing or experimental music or any other less-than-conventional passion, I would want to make sure that kid understood how the world works. I'd want them to know that at some point, Mom and Dad are going to want to reclaim that childhood bedroom and use it for a home office. The kid's going to have to make a living. I wouldn't want someone to wake up on his thirty-fifth birthday mad at the world because he can't afford a new car on a skateboarding income. And that can happen. It can lead to depression.

But so can doing something you hate for the sake of a salary. If a kid wants to be a rock 'n' roll star, what's the harm in going after it? I would advise such a kid to stay in school and get good grades so that if he eventually decides to try another path, he'd have options open. I'd ask him whether he'd be happy if it turned out that he never made it big and wound up playing gigs in small-town bars. I'd ask him if he's prepared to hold down another job so he can feed himself while he pursues his dream. If the answers to those questions were all yes, then I'd advise the kid to go for it and chase excellence in his chosen field.

I understand that the values of the Millennial Generation may differ from the values of their elders. I've always thought that a wonderful part of the American story was the ability of each generation to have more than the generation before it had—college instead of high school, two cars instead of one, a bigger house, and so on. People today may think differently. They may choose to live very modestly and simply for the sake of doing something they love. They may choose not to have children for the sake of being free to work at something that doesn't produce much income. They may choose to forgo the big house, the second car, the lavish vacations. And that, too, is a wonderful part of the American story. No one can force life decisions on you. You make your own life. I can live with any choice that someone makes as long as they have forthrightly considered the consequences of that choice.

I can also admire someone who sees things differently, who decides, ultimately, that the first priority is making enough money to have a family and provide for the children, to educate them well, to give them a nice home to live in. I know lawyers who play in amateur rock bands with other lawyers at night and on weekends, for charity. I know good amateur golfers who once dreamed of playing on the pro tour but decided to become home builders or store managers. They remind me of the sorts of role players that any great team must have. These may be basketball players who dreamed they would be great scorers. But at a certain level, they realized that their abilities were best suited to less glamorous roles—defense and rebounding. They would make their contributions to the team in those ways, and their scoring would be an afterthought. They might be pitchers who started in high school and college, who were the aces of their staffs, but have to become relief pitchers in the big leagues. They may be people like John Calipari, who started out thinking they were going to be great basketball players, then realized their true talent lay in coaching.

Whatever transition they made, they were people of true talent, the talent to be enthusiastic about a role they didn't start out wanting to play.

Doing What You Love or Loving What You Do?

The reality of life is that even if you're blessed with the opportunity to do something you've always loved, there are likely to be parts of the job you don't like. I love my job; that is, I love helping people succeed. But doing that job means I have to travel a lot, and as anyone who travels a lot can tell you, airports and planes and hotel rooms get old very quickly. I have to work very hard to love being in an airport. I do it by focusing on the fun and satisfaction I'm going to have when I reach my destination.

It's important to remember that an individual chooses the attitude he will have. A champion understands that when he's asked to play a role he wouldn't choose under ideal circumstances, he's responsible for the attitude that he brings to that role. He accepts the fact that he's going to take his satisfaction from the knowledge of how many points the man he was guarding didn't score. He accepts the fact that in order to provide for the wife and children he cherishes, he's going to have to be enthused about lawyering, or barbering, or accounting, or whatever his vocation might be. He might, in the back of his mind, be thinking that in ten or twenty or thirty years he's going to build an accounting firm, or a law practice, or a barbershop so successful that he'll be able to sell it for a lot of money. And then he'll follow his original passion. But in the meantime, his pride will make him want to do the best work he can, and he's going to be smart enough to figure out ways to get enthused about that work.

A champion also figures out ways to stay passionate about his life's pursuit, and that's not always easy. I was working with an LPGA player some time ago, and she told me that tournament golf felt, to her, like being in an abusive relationship with a man. I asked her to explain.

"If a woman is in an abusive relationship with a man," this golfer said, "every time they go on a date he winds up beating her up, or verbally abusing her, and she goes home crying, or even bruised. But she wakes up the next morning and can't wait to see him again because she loves him so much. She gets up every day thinking it's going to get better, and it never does."

I could see where she was going with this.

"That's the way I feel about golf," she said. "I love the game. I've loved it for years. I wake up every morning with the dream of being a great player, thinking today's going to be my day, that this is the week I'm going to turn it around. And by the seventh hole, I've had the stuffing beaten out of me, and I go back to my hotel room crying and devastated. But by the time I wake up the next morning, I can't wait to go practice again."

Tournament golf, as this player had discovered, is a demanding dream. She was not unsuccessful; she'd won a few tournaments. But she was becoming aware of how much she had sacrificed to get as far as she had. She was in her early thirties, and she'd sacrificed the normal social and dating life of her peers. "I haven't had a date since the junior prom," she told me. She felt lonely and unloved.

It's not my role to tell people like this golfer what they should do with their lives. I didn't in this case. But I could see that if this young woman wanted to continue to pursue her dream of being a great golf champion, maintaining her passion for the game was going to be a problem.

That is often the case, whether the dream is golf greatness or tremendous success in anything from business to sculpture. If the dreams and goals of exceptional people were easy to realize, people wouldn't have to be exceptional. Anyone could be a great athlete, a bestselling author, or a titan of business. Since their dreams and goals are in fact not easy to attain, many people who want to achieve great things have to struggle. I have clients who dreamed of winning major championships, worked very hard, and then won them. I have more clients who dreamed of winning major championships, worked very hard, and are still struggling on lesser tours or worried about holding on to their PGA Tour playing privileges, or frustrated by their inability to break through and win a major. Staying enthusiastic is a challenge for them. Similarly, I work with clients in the financial world who have to deal with a lot of rejection. In their line of work, the majority of the sales calls they make are destined to be unsuccessful. Rejection can erode enthusiasm and passion, just as the ocean's waves can erode a beach. Not every wave causes a visible amount of sand to wash away. But over time, the beach can disappear.

Sometimes, disenchantment sets in because an individual stops seeing improvement. The real elixir for these people may not be the endeavor itself. It might not, for instance, be the golf. It might be the satisfaction of improving at golf. Improvement can come steadily and rapidly in an individual's youth. But as time goes by, the improvement curve almost invariably flattens out. In golf and other sports, the body starts to age and just won't do the things it did when the athlete was young. I've seen golfers lose their zest for the game when they can't see improvement. I've seen others tear their games apart. They constantly seek the coach or the swing fix that will set them back on the upward curve of improvement. Instead, their games get worse. It's not so easy to love the game when you're not getting better at it.

And the world isn't going to stand still. I've seen talented people lose their passion and enthusiasm because they started dwelling on the changes that have occurred in their business since they were young, changes they don't like. There are veteran college basketball coaches, for instance, who came into coaching when recruiting involved cultivating relationships with the players, their parents, and their high school coaches. But in recent years, a lot of new actors have come along to complicate the recruiting process—AAU coaches and summer camp organizers, to name two. There isn't anything necessarily wrong with this, but it's different. And some college coaches who once were quite good at recruiting have decided they can't stand dealing with these interlopers. Their passion wanes, and so does the ranking of their teams.

Sometimes, people lose their passion because they've made the money they always wanted. I've got nothing against using money as a motivator. Some people in business see their income the way players on the PGA Tour see their score on the tournament leaderboard. They want to be first among their peers, just as Tour players want to be atop the leaderboard. So if they find out that someone at Company A is making X, they want their salary to be $x + 10$ percent. If the desire to make $x + 10$ percent causes them to work very hard and succeed, good for them.

But I've seen cases where people lose their enthusiasm once they reach a financial goal. The most famous example was Byron Nelson. Byron played tournament golf not so much because he loved it or wanted to be the best of all time. He played it because he wanted to be wealthy enough to buy a nice ranch in Texas. Every time he won a tournament, he saw the winner's check as another payment on his dream. It might buy a certain number of acres, or a tractor, or some cattle. And when he got enough money to buy the ranch, he realized very quickly that his enthusiasm for competition had gone. Wisely, he retired from the Tour, even though he was still one of the best players in the world. In every professional sport, general managers can tell you stories about players whose enthusiasm, passion, and talent waned once they signed the big contract that set them up for life.

Pat Bradley, as I've noted, worked with me during the years she was the best player in women's golf. While she was still competing, she qualified for the LPGA Hall of Fame. She invited my wife, Darlene, and me to the installation and banquet at the Ritz-Carlton in Boston. Just before the dinner I saw her in the lobby.

"We've got to talk, Doc," she said.

"What about?" I asked.

"About where we go from here," she said. "I need a new dream, a new goal. I've got to find something to get me up in the morning, you know?"

I understood. Pat loved golf, but even more than that, she had a passion for driving herself to reach a goal that no one else thought she could reach. No one had thought a girl from ski country in New England, a girl without national amateur championships, a girl who didn't hit it a long way, could play golf well enough to get into the LPGA Hall of Fame. Pat loved proving them wrong.

When she was inducted into the LPGA Hall of Fame, it was as if the golf world had said, "You were right and we were wrong, Pat." Pat was wise enough to know she'd need something new to be passionate about. She was forty in the year she entered the Hall of Fame, so it was probably inevitable that she would win less in the years that followed. The mind can't stop the aging process, though it can at times compensate for it. But Pat won only once, in 1995, after making the Hall of Fame. She has found new passions in her life—she's one of the players lobbying the United States Golf Association for a senior women's open, which seems to me only fair. But none of these new passions burn as hot as the one that propelled her in the prime of her career.

Pat built a record to be proud of while her passion was strong, and that distinguishes her from people who "burn out" before they've achieved much of anything. I use the quotations around the term because I don't really believe in burnout. I think people who say they've burned out have in fact chosen to have a negative attitude. Every job comes with its annoying aspects. For me it's travel. For a teacher, it might be students who misbehave or won't do their homework. For a writer, it might be the critics who don't understand her work and write negative reviews—or, worse, ignore it entirely. When someone says he's burned out, I am reminded of people in the midst of a divorce. They're focusing on all the negative aspects of their spouses, when all the positive aspects are still there. They've just chosen to see the spouse differently. They prefer to say they've fallen out of love, because that sounds better to them than saying they've chosen to dwell on the aspects of the spouse they don't like.

If the issue is not a spouse but a job, then an individual who feels burned out has two options. He can decide that he's going to renew his passion for the work by reminding himself of the things he loves about it. Or he can change jobs.

I understand that the latter option can be the better one. I know there are coaches who are turnaround specialists. They love taking the reins at a program that has been steadily unsuccessful. They love making the changes that will turn the program around. They love succeeding where others have failed. But once those changes are made and the program is successful, they find they don't love doing the things needed to maintain success. They love the turnaround process but not the maintenance process. So they quit and get another job. I understand that, although I empathize with the kids and the schools left behind. I know there are turnaround specialists in the business world, and I understand why they would leave their jobs as well. This is healthy, far healthier than staying at a job you no longer love for the sake of a paycheck and turning in a diminished performance because you don't like going to work anymore.

When anyone asks me about quitting a job and trying

something else, I always ask whether the passion is still there. Do you love it still? Do you love it despite the annoying things like the travel? If you do, then the only reason I can see that would impel you to quit is a family obligation. When you have a family and you can't afford to support it on, say, the earnings of a player on the minitours of golf or the earnings of an itinerant rock 'n' roll singer, it's always honorable to find a way to make enough money to fulfill that obligation. And if you love your family, that can be enough.

But as Ralph Waldo Emerson once said, nothing great has ever been accomplished without enthusiasm. Somewhere and somehow, exceptional people find a way to bring that enthusiasm to what they do, and they find it every day.

17.

Sticking with Your Bread and Butter

ONE OF the places you can see exceptional talent at work is the Champions Tour, for players over the age of fifty. They may no longer be the world's best players. Age inevitably takes a little bit away from an individual's power every year. But the players who make it to that Tour, then stay on it and win on it are as good as anyone at one of the tougher virtues to acquire. They stick with what works.

There's a reason why you often see sizable entourages of coaches accompanying a player to the practice tee at a regular Tour event, while for the most part, on the Champions Tour, you see just the player and his caddie. Players on the regular Tour include a lot of seekers. They're young guys who are constantly trying to tweak their swings in an effort to get better. Sometimes this works for them. Often it doesn't. The player tweaks and tweaks, goes through coach after coach, and winds up worse than he was when he started the process.

The mainstays on the Champions Tour tend to know better. They may not have the sort of swing that golf magazines feature. Their swings, in fact, tend to be a little unorthodox and look a little homemade. They don't care. They stick with what has worked for them.

If you look at the guys who were outstanding on the Champions Tour, you'll see names like Don January, Gene Littler, Lee Trevino, Miller Barber, Bernhard Langer, and Hale Irwin, as well as Arnold Palmer and Jack Nicklaus. Some of them, like Littler, had what were perceived as classic swings. But others, like Trevino, had idiosyncratic swings. The only thing they had in common was they weren't overly technical about golf. They had a method that they'd proven worked for them. They didn't care much if anyone else liked it. They weren't into swing overhauls. They stuck with their bread and butter.

That's a tough virtue to acquire, because it seems to conflict with two other virtues, the desire to improve and the desire to be coachable. We're taught that we should always be striving to improve and we should always listen to our coaches. And for a certain period in a person's life, that's good advice. Youngsters almost invariably need to refine their techniques. They shouldn't be satisfied with the skills they have. And they should listen to the right coaches.

The trick is in knowing when that approach becomes counterproductive. I work with a young player who can, unfortunately, serve as an example of the wrong approach. He was a very successful player as an amateur, winning on both the collegiate and national amateur levels. He turned pro. I thought he had the physical skills to win if he learned to think as well as he played, to make the right decisions, to stay with his routine and his process in all situations. He hit the ball a long way, generally with a nice, tight draw off the tee. He wasn't always the most accurate driver, but he didn't need to be. He was good with his scoring clubs, his wedges, and his putter. A long hitter who can also hit the wedges close and putt the ball well doesn't need to be all that accurate off the tee these days. If you can hit it 350 yards and have a short iron into every par-four green, you don't need to play from the fairway to score well. You can make birdies from the rough.

But my young friend was a seeker, which is to his credit. He wanted to get better. He had a lot of people offering him advice. He listened. He heard that he needed to be more accurate with his driver, and that he could hit more fairways if he learned to play a little fade. As Lee Trevino famously opined, "You can talk to a fade, but a hook won't listen." It's an article of faith among touring pros that a fade sits down quickly when it hits the ground and is more likely to stay on the fairway. There's probably some truth to it, though I don't think that the difference is so great that you can't play winning golf with a consistent draw. I've seen too many players do it. But my young client decided to make the change.

Now, most players at the PGA Tour level can turn the ball both ways most of the time. That is, if they're standing on the range and you ask them to show you a draw, they can do it. And if you then ask them to show you a fade, they can do that. On the range. But it's also true that most of them have a bread-and-butter shot off the tee, whether it's a draw or a fade. And in clutch situations, on the golf course, a player tends to rely on his bread-and-butter tee shot. My young client, trying to revamp his natural draw and turn it into a fade, deprived himself of his bread-and-butter shot.

Soon, I found him scared of his driver. He was trying to make his swing less upright and more around his body. He was trying to change his trajectory and hit the ball higher. He was fighting it. When he hit the ball properly, it was impressive. But when he missed, the ball could go anywhere. His misses used to leave him in the rough. As he revamped his swing, they got wilder and wilder. He blocked some. He pulled others. He got very sensitive about remarks he heard about his driving. One fellow pro rather nastily said, "I couldn't break one hundred if I were hitting it where you're hitting it." The guy may have meant it as a backhanded compliment to my client's ability to scramble and save pars, but it wasn't taken that way.

I took him out to play a practice round in Florida and had him hit four or five drives on every hole. He hit nearly all of them well until we got to the final hole, which is a hole a player with a Tour pro's length probably ought to play with a three-wood off the tee. But he hit driver and mishit a couple. The next thing I knew, the driver was flying through the air and into the woods.

We sat down in the clubhouse. "I'm unbelievably fragile right now," he said. "My whole game has become how well I'm driving it. I've started feeling like I can't even play if I don't start driving it better. I'm trying a different swing thought with every tee shot. I feel like I'm hearing a million different things from my swing coach and other people."

He was. Advice was coming from all sides. In addition to advice from his swing coach, his physical trainer had started telling him he needed to work out in the gym more because his weak core muscles were breaking down when he hit the ball hard off the tee. His caddie was trying to get him to hit fairway woods off the tee on holes where he felt he ought to be able to hit driver. And his agent was talking about finding a new swing coach.

"At times I want to give the whole world the bird and just go hide somewhere on an island and live in peace by myself with no one telling me what to do," he said. "Doc, I can't work any harder than I'm working. This last year, I've been more dedicated and put in more hours than I ever have in my life, and I've always been pretty dedicated."

There wasn't much I could tell him about what to do with his driver. Swing mechanics are not my department. I reminded him that when he had played his best golf, he'd also been having fun—going out at night, dating, enjoying himself. Now he was sitting in his room at night, brooding about his driver. He was worried too much. I suggested that he stay in Florida for a while and try to recapture that attitude rather than immediately returning to competition. But that's not easy for a touring pro who has commitments to tournament sponsors, to his equipment companies, and to all the people in his entourage who expect him to play. I hear from him periodically. Sometimes he feels he's very close to hitting his driver the way he wants to. Sometimes he's been missing cuts. I don't know how his story will turn out, but I do know one thing:

I wish he'd stuck to his bread and butter.

I know that's hard for a young golfer today. There's so much information available to players. They see new statistical analyses of their games every day. They see their swings on video all the time. A lot of them have a device called the TrackMan that sits on the range next to them and delivers twenty-six "data points" about every swing they make. They can know the launch angle, clubhead speed, and spin rate of every shot they hit. The chimera of a perfect, powerful, repeating golf swing seems to hover at the end of the range. I see players win major championships and decide that the five-year exemption that goes with winning one will afford them the time they need to work all the messy kinks out of their action. I want to say, "You just won a major championship. How messy could those kinks be?"

I've never worked with Tiger Woods, so I don't know why he's changed his swing coaches and his mechanics as often as he has. I can only think that constantly changing his swing, at least in some ways, has been a mistake. It required that he practice more, and that could be a factor in the physical problems he's been having. I do know that the swing he had when he was in his early twenties seemed to me a pretty good swing. I would have stuck with it.

That is, essentially, what Jack Nicklaus did during his career. He was a much more efficient golfer. He didn't have to hit balls all day. He kept the game very simple. He stayed with the swing he learned from Jack Grout for his entire competitive career. I believe that's a big reason he won major titles well into his forties.

But Jack, as I've noted, has an unusually strong mind. When the final history of his career is written, I hope that his biographer will give Nicklaus's mind as much credit as he gives to Jack's body and golf swing. Jack sought help with his fine points once in a while; he asked Phil Rodgers for help with his chipping and pitching, which was the strongest part of Rodgers's game and the weakest part of Jack's. But for the most part, he listened only to Jack Grout. He never revamped his fundamentals. Instead, he went to Grout once a year for a refresher course that made sure he was doing things the same way he'd been taught to do them when he was a boy. I never met Bob Jones, but from what he wrote, he had that in common with Nicklaus. He learned his swing by watching and imitating a pro named Stewart Maiden, and he never fundamentally changed it.

Obviously, it helped that both Jones and Nicklaus had success early in their careers; success validates technique. If a player is floundering and he has an unorthodox grip, I would never suggest that he stick with that grip.

Nor would I suggest to someone in business that he stick with a business model and work practices that haven't proven themselves. If you're working at a firm that hasn't been doing well, and a new CEO comes in and revamps the way the company does business, it would be foolish to dig in your heels and resist trying what the new boss is asking. On the other hand, if you're a CEO or an established producer and you've been having success doing things a certain way, you'd be foolish to throw that away because some consultant comes along and says you should.

There's a happy medium between listening to everyone and taking all the advice you're offered, and listening to no one and stubbornly hanging on to the same flawed techniques and habits. It's a subtle sweet spot, but it's one that champions seem able to find.

18.

Creating Your Own Reality

ONE OF the concepts I struggle with when I work with people both inside and outside of sport is reality. A golfer may tell me, "Well, being realistic, my goal is just to keep my card this year. Maybe later on, it will be time to think about winning." A recent college graduate might say, "The reality is that the economy is terrible right now and no one is hiring, so I'm just going to live at home and do menial jobs until it gets better."

My job with such people is to get them to understand and believe that exceptional people create their own reality. The average person won't set a goal unless he thinks, and people close to him think, that he has at least a fifty-fifty chance of reaching it. That's what the average person considers a realistic goal. The average person takes account of all the information that's out there saying he can't do something. If, let's say, he thinks about committing himself to becoming the best basketball player he can be and getting a college scholarship, he'll be well aware of the fact that maybe one high school player in thirty gets a college scholarship. Since that seems to make the odds a lot worse than fifty-fifty, the average person is likely to give up on that goal before he even commits to trying to reach it, settling for mediocrity in high school and giving up the game thereafter.

The exceptional person, the person who does great things, doesn't see things that way. The exceptional person has a vision—of great performances, of a great career, of a great something—and doesn't care about what others might say or think. He ignores information that suggests his dream is unrealistic. He just sets about making that vision a reality. He sees things before others see them. He creates his own reality. Afterward, other people may say to him, "We knew you could do it. We always sensed you were going to be one of the great ones." But that's probably not what he heard in the beginning. In the beginning, he probably heard, "You have to be crazy to think you can do that."

In all too many corners of our society, people are placing limits on themselves or accepting the limits others see. I have a friend who teaches in a tough, inner-city high school. The school has an International Baccalaureate program, which is a rigorous set of honors courses. At the end of the program, students take lengthy written exams that are graded outside of the school by an international panel of educators. If a student gets a combined score above a certain number, she is awarded a very prestigious International Baccalaureate diploma in addition to the regular high school diploma.

My friend's school was in danger of losing funds for the program because, for six years, none of the seniors had earned the IB diploma. When he tried to encourage his students to study and prepare for the IB exams, he encountered an attitude best summed up by one of the school's less accomplished students: "Ain't nobody from here be gettin' that diploma."

And that was true. Students from my friend's school were bright enough. But they didn't believe they could earn the diploma, so they didn't study as hard as they might have. On the exams, they doubted themselves. Their essays were tentative and meandering instead of pointed and concise. They sometimes replaced correct answers with incorrect ones. The program had an air of defeat about it. And it remained that way until my friend found two exceptional students. They were exceptional not because they were smarter than anyone else in the school, though they were indeed quite smart. They set themselves apart by refusing to believe they had no chance. Because they believed, they prepared diligently for the exams. And, sure enough, they passed. They created their own reality.

This is analogous to the challenge that faces coaches who take over losing programs and managers who take over departments or companies that have been losing money. It's analogous to the challenge that individuals face when they try to accomplish something that seems to others to be unrealistic.

When a person tells me he's being realistic, I hear a person putting limits on himself. If a golfer tells me his realistic goal is to make a lot of cuts and keep his playing privileges for the next year, I hear him saying that he has decided not to win. He's putting limits on himself. If a financial consultant working for Merrill Lynch or any other company tells me that an annual income of $150,000 is a realistic goal for himself, I hear someone saying that he won't earn more than $150,000, regardless of what his actual potential might be.

I don't have a problem with setting short-term goals that are realistic. If a middle-aged man who's never exercised tells me that he wants to get fit and that to start out, he's going to walk around the block every morning, that's fine with me. That's probably what his physician and a lot of other realists would tell him to do for a start. There's no point in such a person deciding he's going to run five miles the first morning. He almost certainly wouldn't be able to run that far. I don't want him to get discouraged and give up on exercise. But I would not want to hear that person tell me that his dream is to be able to walk around the block. I want his dreams to be unbounded, to be what others would consider unrealistic. I want him to dream about running and winning marathons. His physician might tell him that he's never had a middle-aged patient go from zero exercise to running marathons and that he doesn't think it's possible. Physicians, I guess, are trained to be realists about their patients. But that's not how exceptional people think about themselves. They think about running marathons. Very often, they confound their physicians and everyone else, and they do.

Coaching at the highest level is about getting athletes to believe in things that the experts think are unrealistic. John Calipari used to deal with this issue quite often at the University of Kentucky, because his teams were always loaded with freshmen, and the so-called experts thought they'd need a season or two of experience before they could contend for a title in the Southeastern Conference or the NCAA tournament. (Now that Cal has shown what freshmen are capable of, the experts have changed their view of what's realistic.)

I've helped Cal a little in this. Once or twice a season, I come out to Kentucky to watch the team and talk to them. The best occasions for this are usually after a victory in which the kids haven't played as hard or as well as Cal thinks they can. He can and does lay into them for a substandard effort, but because they've just won, they're a little more receptive. After a loss, athletes tend to withdraw into themselves. If you deliver a message, they'll be quiet, but they won't really be listening.

I tell the players on these occasions that all their skills and all their practice will not be enough when they step on the stage for the big games toward the end of the year that define the success of a Kentucky basketball season. They have to think like champions.

"Don't think you know what's realistic for you and this team," I tell them. "Go out there and create your own reality. Being what most people think is realistic is only a way of justifying negative thinking. Go for something great. Do not settle for good, for almost, or for 'we came close.' Let's go after it, guys."

And I remind them of a truth that John Wooden preached to his players long before they were born. All winners and losers in life are completely self-determined. But only the winners are willing to admit it.

Cal has been creating his own realities for a long time now. Years ago, as a young coach, he took over a mediocre program at the University of Massachusetts. UMass then was a middling school in a conference whose champion got the conference's lone bid to the NCAA tournament and generally lost in the first round. Cal had to set about beating the bushes for players, and one of those bushes was a summer camp. The camp director welcomed Cal and told him he had a good player for him to watch.

So Cal and the camp director went over to a court and watched the player. After ten minutes, Cal had seen enough.

"Sorry, can't use him," Cal said to the camp director.

"What do you mean you can't use him?" the camp director protested. "He'd start for your team right now!"

Cal nodded his head. "Yeah, he'd start for the team we have now," he said. "But he couldn't play for the team we're going to have."

That's creating your own reality.

I sometimes meet with people who tell me that the idea of creating your own reality may work for golfers or basketball players, but it wouldn't work for them. They tell me they're stuck in a job with a company that doesn't pay well, or with a boss who doesn't like them, or in a dying industry. That, they say, is their reality.

I'm sorry. In America, no one is stuck in a job. They choose to remain in that job. I don't care if that job is greeting customers at the door in a Walmart. An individual can choose to do that job so well that he gets promoted to a job that pays more. He can choose to find another job with another company. He can choose to start a business of his own. But if you choose to stay in your present job, you ought to decide you love that job, you're grateful to have it, and you're going to work hard and well at it. That will create more options and new realities for you.

I meet with recent college graduates who tell me the degree they worked for is almost worthless in a bad job market. They tell me their reality is perpetual unemployment or under-employment.

Again, I'm sorry. If a person is facing a tough job market, he can change that reality by being extraordinarily aggressive in his job search. Maybe that's going to some company that has job openings and saying, "I'll work the next two months as an unpaid intern and if at the end of two months you're not so amazed with me that you want to hire me, I'll leave quietly." Then, working as an unpaid intern, he can make sure he figures out how to be more productive than anyone else in the building—starting earlier, working later, getting noticed in a positive way. He can help the company make more money. Yes, it's a tough job market. But companies rarely are so stupid that they get rid of people who improve their earnings.

Successful coaches start out that way all the time. They don't begin with big-time programs knocking on their doors offering them big salaries. They begin as unpaid student assistants, and they work their tails off. They help their teams win. Schools and pro teams, like companies in other sectors, may do stupid things sometimes. But they're rarely stupid enough to get rid of someone who helps them win more. Rather, they identify and cultivate those people.

It's almost as if exceptional people belong to a secret club. In this club, the members know that the average person limits himself. They know that the exceptional person is exceptional in large part because he doesn't limit himself.

I don't know Lady Gaga, but I know she is a member of this club. She told *Rolling Stone* a while back that she operates from a place of delusion. That, to her, is what fame is all about. Back when she was still Stefani Germanotta, she used to walk down the street thinking of herself as a star. She certainly didn't pay any attention to what people in her childhood neighborhood might have thought was a realistic aspiration for Stefani Germanotta. She created a persona for herself, and she made that persona a reality. She believes others can do the same. She told her interviewer that she wanted other people to walk around delusional about how great they can be and then to fight so hard for it every day that the delusion becomes the truth.

If she ever decided to quit singing and become a psychologist, she'd be good at it. She knows what she's talking about.

19.

A Life of Going for It

WHEN I counsel golfers, other athletes, or anyone who comes to me hoping to get more out of himself, I often get a sense that the individual is hanging back. He's nodding his head. He's not openly disagreeing with anything I say. But there's something bothering him, something he's reluctant to express, at least initially. It's only after we've worked together for a while that an individual feels comfortable enough to verbalize this hesitation, this doubt. When it is expressed, it often takes the form of this question:

"What if it doesn't work?"

In other words, what if I commit to doing everything you say, and I believe in it, I work very hard at it, and I still don't make it?

It's a good question. The truth is that there are players on the Hooters Tour doing all the right things to succeed at the highest levels of golf. They're committing themselves to being patient, to the right processes, to long, hard hours honing their skills, then trusting those skills on the golf course. Many of them, nevertheless, will not advance beyond the Hooters Tour. Worse, they'll see some preternaturally gifted players who seem to have all the wrong habits zoom past them in the rankings and claim that spot on the Tour they hoped would be theirs.

Life can indeed seem unfair. There's no trophy for the player who worked the hardest; the trophy goes to the player who used the fewest strokes, regardless of how he made that happen.

So why should someone bother trying to be exceptional? Most people don't. Most people never commit themselves to doing anything that offers worse than fifty-fifty odds of success. Most people choose to live lives that are as safe and secure as they can make them. But then, most people don't really think through the human situation. We're blessed with one life, and that's all we can be certain about. They take that one life they're given and they drift through it. Maybe they're satisfied with that.

The people I know who seek to be exceptional would not settle for a safe, secure, and ultimately dull life. They have a different attitude toward their lives, a philosophy that impels them to go in the opposite direction, to seek excellence, to be exceptional. They fully understand that if they decide that their goal is, say, to win several major championships, there's a very strong likelihood that it won't happen. Statistics tell them that. Uncounted millions of people have played golf. Tens of thousands have gotten good enough to be a touring pro or an elite amateur who can aspire to play in major championships. Only forty-four have won more than two. So the odds are easily more than a million to one against winning several. A smart person wouldn't, I hope, go to a racetrack and put his life savings on a million-to-one horse. So why devote the only life you know you'll have to something equally unlikely?

To me, the answer to that question flows from a philosophy that helps me to understand life and my role in it. The roots of that philosophy lie in my faith and my upbringing in Rutland. The two are so intertwined that it's impossible for me to separate them.

One of the first lessons I remember from Rutland is one my dad taught me, and it's one that I suppose might seem odd coming from someone who has spent so much of his working life helping athletes. My dad taught me that sports are just a means to an end. "Bob," he would say, "sports are short-term. Education is where it's at. If you want to have a good life, you'd better do well in school. Education will give you opportunities. I'm glad you're enjoying sports and having a good time and making progress. But education is way more important."

It turned out that I used my educational opportunities to make my way into a career of coaching and counseling people who want to go for greatness. It happens that many of them are athletes. But I have never wavered in my belief in what my dad said. The scores of games are soon consigned to dusty record books. The trophies won are, in the end, just souvenirs. The lessons we learn in sport are supposed to be what endures. We are supposed to learn from coaches who demand excellence from us that we are capable of more than we first think.

We are supposed to learn about perseverance, and commitment, and confidence, then apply those lessons to the rest of our lives. That's a bedrock principle in my philosophy.

It saddens me when I see athletes graduate from college and then demonstrate that they can't transfer what they learned on the field to their lives after sport. It's one of the great blemishes on American sports that this happens so often. I wish I could sit down with every coach in every sport and talk about how to make sure his athletes are transferring what they learn from him to their other activities.

I was fortunate, I know, because in addition to the coaches in my life, I had parents who worked very hard to make sure I learned the right lessons from my sports and transferred them to my life. And if there was ever a moment when my mom and dad weren't making sure I understood this, the slack was quickly taken up by my teachers and the church.

I certainly don't believe that you have to be religious to have an exceptional life. I know plenty of exceptional people who aren't people of faith. I imagine that a successful atheist must have decided that his life is his complete responsibility. He's probably decided that there's no afterlife, so he's got to make the most of the here and now. Those can be very useful concepts. But some of the best coaches I know of were spiritual men. Joe Gibbs was very single-minded about winning, but he takes a part of every week to discuss faith with a men's group. Vince Lombardi went to Mass every day. John Calipari does the same.

The religious tenets I learned as a boy were very conducive

to leading an exceptional life. The nuns and priests taught us that God had endowed all of us with certain talents, and it was our job to develop them to the highest degree we possibly could. It didn't matter what those talents were. In my teachers' eyes, talent with the clarinet, or a flair for drawing or fixing things, or solving equations, was just as precious and valuable as talent for shooting a basketball. All of them had to be developed. If you got clarinet lessons and showed some ability, it was important to join the school band. And if you joined the band, it was important to strive to become first clarinetist.

They recognized, of course, that there was a little more local celebrity attached to being the starting pitcher for the school's baseball team than to being first clarinetist. That's the nature of American culture, for better or worse. But they took pains to tell those of us who were athletes that this didn't mean we were better or more important than anyone else. It only meant we had a few additional obligations. We had to be pleasant and friendly with everyone. Since little kids looked up to us, we had to be certain we set a good example. We were taught that you weren't going to heaven because you made a lot of money. You weren't even going to heaven if you gave all your money to the church. Your eternal life depended on how well you treated other people. And on how you developed your God-given gifts by using the free will that God also gave you. I think that's the way a religious person views life. Vince Lombardi used to tell his players that family, religion, and team had to be the three most important things in their lives—in that order. He told them that if they did not commit themselves to being the best players they could be, they were cheating themselves and wasting their talents.

I have always accepted the idea that belief in God is a matter of blind faith. In fact, I very much like that idea. I like the idea that even though I can't see God, I can firmly believe in His existence and in His role in my life. I'm not going to argue with anyone who doesn't have that faith. I'm not going to debate, and I really don't care what other people believe. I like the idea because it reinforces for me the importance and power of faith. Just like belief in God, belief in the ability to do extraordinary things is a matter of faith, at least initially. And I like the way faith has influenced me in the way I treat my wife, my parents, my brothers and my sister, my family and friends and the people I do business with. I like the way faith has influenced my belief in my abilities. I like the way faith has influenced the achievements of people I counsel.

I think having faith and believing that things are ultimately in God's hands is very close to trusting your ability in sports such as golf. When a golfer is in the right frame of mind, he's confident that he can produce the shot he sees with his mind's eye. He trusts that the skills he has ingrained through practice are going to work for him if he just lets them and doesn't try to guide or steer the ball. But at the same time, part of his thinking is acceptance of whatever happens to the golf ball once he hits it. He knows that because he's a human being, not every shot will come off the way he intends it. He knows that because golf can be a capricious game, his ball is sometimes going to take a weird hop into the woods.

He knows he can only do his best and wait to see what the outcome is. To me, that's very similar to a person of faith believing that if he does his human best, he can trust in God to make sure things turn out for the best in the long run, whether that long run plays out in this life or the next.

John Wooden captured the affinity between religion and a philosophy of exceptionalism in his Pyramid of Success. Wooden was a very spiritual man, but he coached at public universities and he believed in the separation of church and state. So he never proselytized with his players. Instead, he taught them principles that would help them make the best of their talents, both as basketball players and as men. The blocks of the pyramid—things like honesty, patience, integrity, cooperation, and self-control—are not very much different from the virtues I remember being taught during religious instruction.

Another outstanding coach, Dick Bennett, had a similarly spiritual approach with his teams. Dick was highly successful at the University of Wisconsin and other schools; his son, Tony, is building an equally successful record now as coach at the University of Virginia. Dick told his players he wanted his teams to build their skills on five pillars—humility, passion, unity, servanthood, and thankfulness.

Those could be the tenets of a religious order as well as a basketball team. But in the end, it doesn't matter where a philosophy that promotes exceptionalism comes from. It can come either from religion or from a thoughtful consideration of the circumstances of human existence. But it needs to come from somewhere.

Once an individual has a philosophy, he should be ready to answer the question "What if I fail?" He should understand that over the span of a lifetime, the only lasting failure is the failure to try. He appreciates the opportunity to find out what he can do with his life and career. He understands that he has been blessed with some God-given abilities and with free will. Free will allows him to choose what to do with those abilities. He can strive to develop them to the fullest possible extent. He can choose to enjoy the challenge of pressing the limits of his human potential. Or he can choose to let his God-given gifts lie fallow. He chooses to be accountable and responsible for the development of his gifts.

He cares about the results he achieves to some extent, because those results can be a good gauge of the effort he invested. But he knows that the effort is more important than the results. He knows there can be games where the scoreboard says he won, but in his heart he knows that he didn't, because he didn't meet his standards for effort, whether they involve rebounding and diving for loose balls or putting all the heart and soul he has into a violin solo or building a house where every nail is hammered precisely. Regardless of what others might think or say, he defines exceptional for himself. He wants very much to be proud of the effort he made every day. He wants to spend his time seeing whether he can get a little bit better at whatever it is that he chooses to do.

He understands, of course, that he can't do this alone. He needs the help of others—his spouse, his parents, his family, his coaches, his teammates. He measures himself, in part, by how much he contributes to the lives of these people and others.

I see this desire to help others manifest itself in many ways in the lives of exceptional people. John Calipari makes certain that his Kentucky players make lots of visits to schools and hospitals throughout the year. He knows that the kids in the schools and the patients in the hospitals live in Kentucky, so they're likely to be thrilled by a visit from a Kentucky player. He wants his players to understand the importance of giving something back and the personal satisfaction that comes from doing so. At the University of Virginia, we have a very successful alumnus, Paul Tudor Jones, who has made a lot of money in the New York financial and trading world. He's poured a lot of it back into the Robin Hood Foundation, which attacks poverty in New York City. That's what I think Earl Woods was getting at when he helped Tiger start a foundation very early in his career to build learning centers for kids who needed them. I know that's what the nuns back in school were getting at when they let us know that while they were happy when we won football games, that success only meant something if it spread faith by bearing witness to living a life of godliness.

A good philosophy incorporates humility. A person with the right philosophy does not think he's more entitled than anyone else. He doesn't feel bigger, better, or more important than anyone else. If he is entitled to any special consideration, it's because of the things he's done, not simply who he is. If I had to give an example, I might use Paul McCartney and Prince Charles of England. Paul McCartney, from everything I know, is a very down-to-earth individual. I'm sure he feels entitled to a certain respect for the great songs he's written and the pleasure they have brought to millions of people. But that's it. Prince Charles, on the other hand, embodies the concept of entitlement by virtue of birth. He may well be a down-to-earth individual, for all I know. But if you asked a person with a philosophy of exceptionalism whether he'd rather be Paul McCartney or Prince Charles, Paul McCartney would be the answer.

A good philosophy appreciates competition and fellow competitors. Competition teaches us about ourselves. It pushes and pulls us to try things we might not try and change things we might not change in the absence of competition. It would be very hard to chase excellence if you didn't have competitors who wanted it as badly as you did. You can see this in virtually any endeavor. I saw it when Tiger Woods burst into professional golf. Players stepped up their games and their training regimens to compete with him. I suspect you could have seen it in France in the 1870s when Claude Monet showed his first impressionist painting of a sunrise on the Seine. Renoir and the others thought, "Whoa! I've got to step up my game." And they did.

The media generally try to turn an on-the-field rivalry into some sort of grudge match or hatred. In my experience, it rarely is. I think most athletes wind up liking the people they compete with to the extent that they know them. You have only to watch the telecast of a baseball game to see this. When a player for the Yankees reaches first base against the Red Sox, he's likely to have a pleasant little conversation with the first baseman. This doesn't mean the Yankees don't want to beat the Red Sox, and vice versa. They do. But they also realize that their sport would not exist without competition, and they appreciate the effort the opposition puts into chasing the same goal they're chasing.

The media also like to misrepresent Vince Lombardi when they talk about competition and competitors. Lombardi did indeed post a sign on the locker room wall one time saying, "Winning isn't everything. It's the only thing." But my cousin Sal Somma, who knew Lombardi well from their days competing and coaching against one another in the New York area, said that when he and Lombardi did clinics together Lombardi would bemoan the way that quote had been ripped out of context and misrepresented. It was presented to the public as if football were war, and the only acceptable outcome was to crush the enemy. Lombardi said he never meant to denigrate another human being based on whether or not they won a football game. His old players, when asked, remember that they could lose to a superior opponent, and if they had given their best effort, Lombardi would pat them on the back and say he was proud of them. At other times, they remember being chewed out after defeating an inferior opponent if their effort did not meet Lombardi's standards. It was the effort that mattered to him, not the outcome. The Lombardi they remember was a prophet of personal excellence. He taught them that sustaining a commitment to personal excellence over a lifetime would separate them from other people and make them exceptional.

There's a cliché about the destination being less important than the journey. Sometimes ideas become clichéd because people find them worth repeating over and over again. Exceptional people really do come to believe that the journey is more important than the destination. It's another way of saying that the effort is more important than the outcome. John Calipari worked and scrapped for years to build a team that could win an NCAA championship. When he finally did it, he told me that winning the title wasn't quite the big deal he'd always dreamed it would be. Other people thought it was, but Cal didn't. He found that what really satisfied him was the daily process of becoming a champion—the recruiting, the practicing, getting kids to believe in his system and come together. That was the real reward, and he was looking forward to starting it all over again with a new crop of prospects.

The title was nice, but in the end he realized that luck plays a role in the outcome of any competition. I think any competitor who's honest with himself comes to the same conclusion. There are coaches who have great careers, do all the right things, but don't win an NCAA championship because, at the worst possible moment, a key player got injured. There are golfers who come within a stroke of winning a major and don't get it because a couple of putts lip out or a gust of wind blows the ball off line. Conversely, most players who have won majors will tell you that in addition to everything they did right that week, it seemed like all the bounces went their way and all the putts on the lip fell in. Once in a while, someone is so dominating—like Tiger Woods at the U.S. Open in 2000, which he won by fifteen strokes—that he can honestly say luck had nothing to do with his triumph. Most of the time, though, an honest competitor understands that he could just as easily have lost. Some baseball teams get hot at the right time—in September and October. They don't plan it; they're trying to be hot all season. They might not replicate it the next season. But it happens, and they win the World Series. Or, on the other side of the equation, they run into a team that's, for the moment, hotter still, and they lose the World Series.

The honest competitor understands that while luck affects outcomes, it doesn't affect effort. So he learns to take his pleasure from the daily grind. He understands that life is sometimes going to break his heart. He may work as hard as he possibly can and still not get the promotion or the sale. He may go on a mission to improve his free-throw shooting or his short game and still chunk the chip that makes the difference between winning and losing the club championship. He may pour his heart into a screenplay and never see it produced because someone else made a film that was vaguely similar and it flopped at the box office. He decides to take his satisfaction from the effort he produces every day, and because he controls his attitude, he gets enormous pleasure from it. He may or may not win ultimate prizes—the championship, the CEO job, the Oscar—but because he has chosen an endeavor that he loves and has talent for, he sees progress every day. He's proud of that. He's happy with that.

Viewed in that perspective, life for anyone living in a country like America, a country blessed with peace and prosperity, can be a never-ending treat. You get a chance to see how good you can be at something you love doing. You get to have a ball for many years seeing how many wonderful things you can do with your life.

On top of that, you'll be blessed with peace of mind. You'll be calm and composed when things aren't going well. You'll handle the good things with grace. You'll find that in crises, things slow down. You'll have the sense that the world is your home court. You'll be comfortable competing there. When you retire, you'll like the face you see in the mirror. You'll go on to the next phase of your life and look for new things to learn, new things to do. And on your last day, you'll look back and think how lucky you were to have lived the life you did.

That's how champions think.

ABOUT THE AUTHORS

Dr. Bob Rotella was the director of sports psychology at the University of Virginia for twenty years, during which time his reputation grew as the person champions talked to about the mental aspects of their game. His client list includes the winners of more than seventy major championships in men's, women's, and senior golf; star athletes in all other major sports including tennis, baseball, basketball, and football; singers, rock stars, and other artistic performers; and business leaders at companies such as Merrill Lynch, General Electric, Ford, and Coca-Cola. Dr. Rotella lives in Virginia with his wife, Darlene.

Bob Cullen is a journalist and writer. During the years he has collaborated with Dr. Bob Rotella, his golf handicap has gone from 21 to 5. He lives with his wife, Ann, in Chevy Chase, Maryland.